Homeowners' Guide to Construction Defects

RYAN BRAUTOVICH

Copyright © 2013 Ryan Brautovich

All rights reserved. No part of this book may be reproduced or transmitted in any form or by any means, electronic or mechanical, including photocopying, recording, or by any information storage and retrieval system, without the written permission of the Publisher.

Printed in the United States of America

January 2013

ISBN: 978-0-9864404-7-2

"If a building looks better under construction than it does when finished, then it's a failure."

~ Doug Coupland

The Construction H.E.L.P. Foundation's Home Construction Audit program makes it easy and painless – through the use of our Home Building System – to understand how to build a home, how to manage your contractor, and how to protect yourself from being taken advantage of and scammed. We demystify the process and remove all of the contractor jargon to give you the building process in easy-to-understand, plain English. The Construction H.E.L.P. Foundation's founder and building expert Ryan Brautovich's exclusive 4-step home building system will ensure you are on the right track – and on budget – every step of the way. For more information about the Construction H.E.L.P Foundation, the Home Construction Audit Program, or any of the educational products, homeowner services, or construction seminars available in your area, please visit www.HomeConstructionAudit.com, or www.ConHelp4U.org.

TABLE OF CONTENTS

FOUNDATIONS	1
SLAB ON GRADE	1
CONCRETE FOUNDATION IS CRACKED	1
CONCRETE SLAB IS NOT LEVEL	1
CONCRETE SLAB IS UNEVEN	1
GRADE BEAM AND PIER	2
EXTERIOR FOUNDATION GRADE BEAM IS OUT OF LEVEL	2
FOUNDATION GRADE BEAM IS OUT OF SQUARE	2
EXPOSED WOOD AROUND PIERS OR GRADE BEAMS	2
BASEMENTS AND OTHER BELOW GRADE STRUCTURES	3
WATER TRICKLES INTO BASEMENT OF GARAGE THROUGH WALLS OR FLOOR	3
BASEMENT AND CONCRETE GARAGE WALLS ARE NOT PLUMB	3
BASEMENT AND CONCRETE GARAGE WALLS ARE BOWED	3
BASEMENT WALLS HAVE CRACKS OR HOLES, FLOORS HAVE CRACKS	4
STANDING WATER IN CRAWL SPACE	4
FLOORS AND CEILINGS	4
FLOOR SQUEAKS	4
WOOD SUBFLOORS OR CEILINGS ARE NOT FLAT	5
WOOD SUBFLOORS AND/OR DECKS ARE OUT OF LEVEL	5
WOOD SUBFLOORS HAVE "SPRINGINESS" OR BOUNCE	5
SUBFLOOR IS OUT-OF-SQUARE	5
EXTERIOR WOOD BEAMS OR POSTS ARE WARPED, CRACKED OR SPLIT	6
WOOD BEAMS OR POSTS ARE TWISTED OR CUPPED	6
WALLS	6
STUCCO WALLS	6
CRACKS ON STUCCO WALLS	6
WATER STAINS OR WATER DAMAGE TO INTERIOR WALLS	7
COLOR COAT REPAIR WORK DOES NOT MATCH EXISTING COLOR	7

- WEEP SCREED FLASHING IS RUSTING OR RUST MARKS APPEAR ON NUMBEROUS PLACES ON THE SURFACE OF THE OUTSIDE WALLS   7
- STUCCO COLOR COAT IS SEPARATING FROM THE BROWN COAT   8
- WET SPOTS REMAIN ON STUCCO WALLS AFTER A RAIN STORM   8
- LATH IS VISIBLE THROUGH THE STUCCO   8
- FOAM BOARD IS VISIBLE THROUGH THE STUCCO   8
- WHITE POWDERY SUBSTANCE (EFFLORESCENCE) APPEARS ON STUCCO WALLS IN WINTER MONTHS   8
- WOOD TRIM IS EMBEDDED IN STUCCO   9
- STUCCO WALL APPEARS "WAVY" DURING SUNSET HOURS OR WHEN LIGHTED WITH LANDSCAPE LIGHTS   9
- PLYWOOD BEHIND STUCCO IS DELAMINATING OR SPLITTING   9

EXTERIOR TRIM   10
- THERE ARE GAPS BETWEEN THE HOUSE BODY AND THE EXTERIOR TRIM   10
- EXTERIOR TRIM BOARD IS SPLIT, BOWED, TWISTED, OR CUPPED   10

HARDBOARD SIDING   10
- EXTERIOR SURFACE IS BUCKLED   10
- DRIP EDGE OF LAP SIDING IS SWOLLEN OR SPLIT   11
- SIDING MATERIAL IS SWOLLEN OR SPLIT AROUND NAILS   11
- SIDING SPLITS, SOFTENS, AND ROTS AT THE BASE OF WALLS   12
- BUTT JOINTS ARE TOO WIDE   12
- SIDING IS CROOKED   12
- SIDING IS SOFT AND ROTTING AT WINDOW AND DOOR TRIM, RAILINGS, AND OTHER LOCATIONS   12
- SIDING HAS RAISED NAIL HEADS   13

PANEL SIDING   13
- JOINTS AT PANEL EDGES ARE EXCESSIVELY WIDE OR RAISED   13
- PANELS ARE DELAMINATING   13
- PANELS ARE BOWED   13

VINYL SIDING   14
- VINYL SIDING IS BOWED   14
- VINYL SIDING IS FADED OR BLOTCHED   14

CEMENT BOARD SIDING	14
CEMENT BOARD SIDING IS CRACKED OR CHIPPED	14
INTERIOR WALLS	15
WALLS ARE OUT OF PLUMB	15
WALLS ARE BOWED	15
INTERIOR WALL INTERSECTIONS ARE NOT PERPENDICULAR ON WALLS THAT ARE DESIGNED TO MEET AT 90 DEGREE ANGLES	15
SHEAR WALLS	16
SHEAR WALLS ARE INADEQUATE	16
SHEAR WALLS OR HOLD DOWNS ARE MISSING	16
ROOFS	16
FLASHING	16
FLASHING HAS RUSTED	16
ROOF RIDGE SAGS	17
ROOF SHEATHING IS BOWED	17
SLATE, CONCRETE AND CLAY TILES	17
ROOF LEAKS	17
LOOSE OR FALLING ROOF TILES OR SLATE	18
CHIPPED OR BROKEN ROOF TILES OR SLATE	18
IMPROPER EXPOSURE, LAPPING AND SPACING OF TILES OR SLATE	19
LACK OF ADEQUATE NAILING	19
MISSING OR IMPROPERLY APPLIED SHEET METAL FLASHINGS	19
COMPOSITION ASPHALT SHINGLES	20
ROOF LEAKS	20
SHINGLES HAVE BLOWN OFF	20
SHINGLES ARE NOT HORIZONTALLY ALIGNED	20
SHINGLES ARE CURLED OR CUPPED AT EDGES AND CORNERS	21
SHINGLES OVERHANG EDGES OF ROOF, TOO FAR OR TOO LITTLE	21
ASPHALT SHINGLES HAVE DEVELOPED SURFACE BUCKLING	21
SHADING OR SHADOWING PATTERN APPEARS ON THE SHINGLES	21
EROSION OF SHINGLE SURFACING MATERIALS	22
UNSEALED SHINGLE TABS	22
ROOF VENTILATION	22
ATTIC VENT OR LOUVER LEAKS	22

- EAVES — 23
  - LEAKES OR STAINS APPEAR AT THE UNDERSIDE OF THE EAVES — 23
  - ROOF SAGS OR BOWS AT EAVES AND FASCIA — 23
- BUILT-UP ROOFING AND OTHER LOW SLOPE ROOFS — 23
  - STANDING WATER ON ROOF — 23
  - ROOF LEAKS — 24
  - ROOF MEMBRANE HAS BUBBLES OR BLISTERS — 24
  - ROOF MEMBRANE HAS SPLITS OR TEARS — 25
  - ROOF HAS BARE SPOTS — 25
  - ROOFING MATERIAL AT THE ROOF-TO-WALL INTERSECTION IS SPLITTING — 25
  - UNSEALED LAPS — 26
  - FASTENER BACK-OUT — 26
  - ACCUMULATION OF BROWN RESIDUE FROM ASPHALT ROOFING PRODUCTS — 26
- EXTERIOR COMPONENTS — 27
  - WALKWAYS AND DRIVEWAYS — 27
    - DRIVEWAY IS CRACKED — 27
    - WALKWAY IS CRACKED — 27
    - WATER PONDS ON SIDEWALK — 28
    - CONCRETE DRIVEWAY THAT ABUTS THE GARAGE IS HIGHER THAN THE GARAGE SLAB — 28
    - DRIVEWAY APPROACH IS TOO STEEP, CAUSING VEHICLES TO SCRAP OR TO BOTTOM OUT — 28
    - CONCRETE DRIVEWAY IS SPALLING, SCALING OR CHIPPING — 29
    - CONCRETE STOOP IS PULLING AWAY FROM THE FOUNDATION — 29
  - GARAGE DOORS — 30
    - GARAGE DOOR LEAKS WATER/SNOW AT HEAD, JAMBS OR THRESHOLD — 30
    - GARAGE DOOR FAILS TO OPERATE PROPERLY OR GETS JAMMED — 30
    - GARAGE DOOR "MYSTERIOUSLY" OPENS — 30
  - DECKS AND PATIOS — 31
    - WATER PONDS ON DECKS AND PATIOS — 31
    - DECK MEMBERS ARE ROTTING — 31
    - DECK IS NOT FLASHED AT HOUSE/DECK CONNECTION — 32
    - NAIL HEADS OR SCREWS PROTRUDE ABOVE THE SURFACE OF THE DECK BOARDS — 32
    - PATIO SURFACES CRACK AND SEPARATE — 32

FINISHED CONCRETE SURFACE HAS A BLOTCHY/MOTTLED COLOR	33
WINDOWS AND PATIO DOORS	33
GLASS IS SCRATCHED OR BROKEN	33
GLASS HAS IMPERFECTIONS	34
WINDOWS AND PATIO DOORS ARE DIFFICULT TO OPEN AND CLOSE	34
WINDOW IS FOGGED BETWEEN PANES OF GLASS	34
WINDOW GRIDS DISINTEGRATE	35
WINDOW/PATIO DOOR LEAKS AT TOP OR BOTTOM	35
WINDOWS LEAK WHEN THE WIND BLOWS HARD	35
FRENCH DOORS AND OTHER EXTERIOR DOORS	36
WATER ENTERS WALLS AND INTERIOR THROUGH TOP, JAMBS AND THRESHOLD	36
DOORS ARE WARPED, OUT-OF-LEVEL, NOT PLUMB	36
CORROSION OR STAINING OF EXTERIOR HARDWARE	37
CHIMNEY AND FLUES	37
CHIMNEY CAP DOES NOT DRAIN	37
FLUE ENCLOSURE OPENS FOR ENTIRE HEIGHT (THROUGH FLOORS AND CEILINGS)	38
IN THE CHIMNEY, WATER RUNS DOWN THE OUTSIDE OF THE FLUE	38
GUTTERS AND DOWNSPOUTS	39
STANDING WATER IN GUTTERS AFTER RAINFALL	39
GUTTER JOINTS LEAK / DOWNSPOUT JOINTS LEAK	40
GUTTER ENDS ARE EMBEDDED IN WALL SURFACE MATERIAL	40
GUTTERS OVERFLOW	40
GUTTERS DO NOT EXTEND FULLY TO THE GABLE ENDS OF THE ROOF	41
DOWNSPOUT MAKES "PINGING" NOISE DURING RAIN STORMS	41
SKYLIGHTS	42
SKYLIGHT LEAKS	42
MOISUTRE CONDENSES ON INTERIOR SURFACES OF THE SKYLIGHT	42
MOISTURE APPEARS BETWEEN THE PANES OF A DUAL PANE SKYLIGHT	42
SKYLIGHT ADMITS TOO MUCH HEAT	43
PAINT AND STAIN	43
STAINS FROM UNDERLYING SURFACES BLEED THROUGH	43

PAINT BECOMES CHALKS OR FADES	43
PAINT FLAKING OR PEELING	44
PAINTS APPLED TOO THIN, TOO TICK, OR IN A SPOTTY MANNER	44
PAINT OR STAIN OVERSPRAY ON ADJACENT SURFACES	45
MILDEW OR FUNGI GROWTH / STAINS ON PAINTED SURFACES	45
LACQUERS AND VARNISHES PEEL AND FLAKE RAPIDLY	46
STAINED EXTERIOR SURFACES ARE BLOTCHY OR HAVE UNEVEN COLOR	46
PAINTED STUCCO SURFACES DO NOT PERMIT MOISTURE TO ESCAPE	47
BRUSH MARKS OR LAP MARKS SHOW	47
BRICK AND MASONRY	47
CHIMNEY IS CRACKED	47
MASONRY WALL OR MASONRY VENNER IS CRACKED	48
CUT BRICKS BELOW OPENINGS IN MASONRY WALLS ARE DIFFERENT THICKNESS	48
BRICK OR CMU COURSES ARE NOT STRAIGHT AND MORTAR JOINTS VARY IN THICKNESS	48
BRICK IS DISINTEGRATING (SPALLING)	48
INTERIOR COMPONENTS	49
FIREPLACES	49
WATER DRIPS INTO FIREPLACE DURING RAINSTORMS	49
FIREPLACE WON'T DRAW (ROOM BECOMES SMOKY)	49
REFRACTORY PANELS CRACK	50
DAMPER BECOMES DUSTY	50
GLASS DOORS DO NOT OPERATE FREELY	50
INSULATION	51
THERE IS NO INSULATION IN THE ATTIC	51
INSULATION IS PLACED AGAINST THE EAVE VENTS OR THE FOUNDATION VENTS	51
HOUSE IS TOO HOT IN SUMMER, TOO COLD IN WINTER	51
INSULATION BATTS DO NOT FIT TIGHT TO THE FRAMING MEMBERS	52
INTERIOR DOORS	52
DOOR IS WARPED	52
DOOR PANELS HAVE SPLIT	52

DOOR LATCH DOES NOT ENGAGE IN THE STRIKE PLATE	53
DOOR OPENS OR CLOSES BY ITSELF	53
BOTTOM EDGE OF DOOR IS CUT TOO HIGH OR TOO LOW	53
POCKET DOOR BINDS BETWEEN THE POCKETS	54
DOOR HARDWARE	54
DOORKNOB MECHANISM OPERATES STIFFLY	54
DOORKNOB FINISH TARNISHES	54
CLOSETS	55
POLES PULL OUT OF ROSETTES	55
FINISH FLOORING	55
FLOOR NOT LEVEL, FLOOR SQUEAKS, EXCESSIVE DEFLECTION (SAGGING), EXCESSIVE FELEXIBILITY (BOUNCE)	55
HARDWOOD FLOORING	56
CUPPING OR CROWNING OF INDIVIDUAL FLOOR BOARDS	56
SCALLEOPED AND ABRADED SURFACE	56
GAPS BETWEEN ADJACENT FLOOR BOARDS	57
DIFFERENCES IN COLOR BETWEEN INDIVIDUAL FLOOR BOARDS	57
FLOOR BOARDS ON PRE-FINISHED FLOORS ARE NOT LEVEL WITH ONE ANOTHER AT SIDES OR ENDS	58
SPLINTERS OR CHIPS ARE PRESENT AT THE EDGES OF FLOOR BOARDS AFTER INSTALLATION	58
DARK LINES APPEAR PERPENDICULAR TO THE FLOOR BOARD	58
FLOOR BOARDS DISCOLOR AND ROT, PARTICULARLY UNDER AREA RUGS	59
CERAMIC AND CLAY TILE FLOORING	59
CRACKS AND / OR LOOSE TILES	59
GROUT IS CRACKED	59
INDIVIDUAL TILES ARE OUT OF PLANE	60
GRANITE, MARBLE, AND OTHER STONE FLOORING	60
CRACKS	60
STAINS	60
SCRATCHES AND ABRASIONS	61
VINYL FLOORING	61
WIDE SEAMS OR JOINTS	61
DELAMINATION	62
DISCOLORATION	62

ADHESIVE APPEARS ON THE SURFACE THROUGH JOINTS	62
"TELEGRAPHING" OR IRREGULAR SURFACE BEANEATH VINYL FLOORING	63
PATTERN DOES NOT MATCH OR ALIGN	63
CARPET FLOORING	63
VISIBLE SEEMS	63
CARPET IS LOOSE	64
CARPET FIBERS SEPARATE FROM BACKING	64
FADING AND DISCOLORATION	64
CARPET TEXTURE DOES NOT ALIGN AT SEAMS	65
CARPETS HAVE A DARK SOIL LINE AT STAIR AND BASEBOARD EDGES	65
THERE IS A BUMP AT THE TRANSITION BETWEEN CARPET AND HARD SURFACE FLOORING	65
PLASTER AND DRYWALL	66
DRYWALL / PLASTER IS CRACKED	66
DRYWALL HAS NAIL POPS	66
DRYWALL CROWNS IN CEILING, DRYWALL BOWS ON WALLS	67
SURFACE TEXTURE IS UNEVEN OR IRREGULAR	67
COUNTERTOPS	68
COUNTERTOP IS NOT LEVEL	68
BACKSLASH IS LOOSE	68
CERAMIC TILE COUNTERTOPS	68
UNEVEN SURFACE	68
UNEQUAL GROUT JOINTS	69
GROUT JOINT CRACKS	69
CRACKED TILE	69
COLOR AND TEXTURE VARIATIONS	70
LOOSE TILE	70
WATER PENETRATION THROUGH TOP	70
GRANITE, MARBLE, STONE COUNTERTOPS	71
CRACKS	71
TEXTURE AND COLOR VARIATIONS	71
STAINS	71
CHIPS	72
PLASTIC LAMINATE COUNTERTOPS	72
OPEN JOINTS	72
DELAMINATION	73
UNACCEPTABLE TRIMMING	73
STAINS AND BURNS	73
SOLID SURFACE COUNTERTOPS	74

OPEN SEAMS	74
ROUGHENED SURFACE	74
STAINS AND BURNS	75
BLEMISHES AND SCRATCHES	75
CULTURE MARBLE COUNTERTOPS	75
BLEMISHES AND INCONSISTENT COLOR	76
VOIDS AT SURFACE	76
LEAKS AT JOINTS AND FITTINGS	76
APPLIANCES	77
APPLIANCES DO NOT PERFORM AS INTENDED	77
CABINETS AND VANITIES	77
CABINETS DESIGNED TO SET FLUSH WITH THE CEILING HAVE A VISIBLE GAP, SPACE, OR SEPARATION	77
CABINETS ARE NOT *FLUSH* WITH ONE ANOTHER	77
CABINETS ARE WARPED	78
CABINET DRAWER GUIDE HAS BROKEN	78
CABINET DRAWER IS BINDING DURING OPENING	78
CABINET DOOR SWING OPEN AND / OR WILL NOT STAY CLOSED	79
DOORS OR DRAWERS HAVE CRACKS IN THE PANELS	79
PLASTIC LAMINATE SURFACES ARE PEELING AWAY	79
CABINETS DO NOT SIT LEVEL	80
CABINET DOORS DO NOT ALIGN WHEN CLOSED	80
CABINET FINISH (PAINT OR STAIN) IS IRREGULAR, MISMATCHED, OR BLOTCHY	80
GAPS APPEAR BETWEEN SECTIONS WHERE CABINETS ARE JOINED	80
STAIN GRADE CABINETS SHOW A "DARK" BAND AROUND DOOR AND DRAWER OPENINGS	81
STAIRS AND RAILINGS	81
STAIRS HAVE GAPS BETWEEN TREADS, RISERS AND SKIRT BOARDS	81
STAIR TREADS AND RISERS ARE UNEVEN	81
STAIR TREAD DEFLECTS EXCESSIVELY	82
STAIR TREADS SQUEAK	82
STAIR RAILINGS DEFLECT EXCESSIVELY	82
MOLDINGS AND TRIM	82
GAPS APPEAR AT JOINTS	82
NAIL HEADS ARE VISIBLE IN THE FINISHED WOODWORK	83

GAPS OCCUR WHERE MOLDING ABUTS ONE ANOTHER OR ABUTS ANOTHER MATERIAL	83
MOLDING OR TRIM IS SPLIT OR CHECKED	83
HAMMER MARKS OR OTHER MARRS ARE VISIBLE	84
MIRRORS	84
SCRATCHES ON GLASS SURFACE	84
MIRROR BACKING IS DETERIORATING	85
MIRROR WARDROBE DOORS DO NOT HAVE SAFETY BACKING (WALK-IN CLOSETS)	85
SHOWER AND TUB ENCLOSURES	85
GLASS/PLASTIC IS SCRATCHED	85
SHOWER OR TUB ENCLOSURES LEAK	86
FIBERGLASS OR ACRYLIC TUB BOTTOM OR SHOWER STALL ENCLOSURE FLEXES WHEN OCCUPIED	86
SHOWER/TUB ENCLOSURES ARE NOT TEMPERED GLASS	86
TOP RAIL OF SHOWER/TUB ENVLOSURE IS NOT SCREWED TO THE FRAME	87
GROUT IS CRACKED BETWEEN THE TUB/SHOWER AND FIRST ROW OF TILE	87
WATER RESISTANT BACKING IMPROPERLY INSTALLED AT TUB OR SHOWER SURROUNDINGS	87
UTILITY SYSTEMS	88
HEATING	88
SOME ROOMS ARE COMFORTABLE, WHILE OTHER ROOMS ARE COLD	88
THERMOSTAT DOES NOT WORK	89
SYSTEM IS NOISY WHEN OPERATING	89
HEATING SYSTEM MAKES BOOMING NOISE WHEN FIRST TURNED ON, OR WHEN COOLING DOWN	89
HEATING SYSTEM MAKES BOOMING NOISE WHEN FIRST TURNED ON	89
COLD SPOTS DEVELOP ON THE FLOOR (RADIANT SYSTEM)	90
DUCT WORK HAS SEPARATED	90
COOLING	91
AIR CONDITIONER DOES NOT COOL THE HOUSE	91
SOME ROOMS ARE HOTTER (OR COLDER) THAN OTHERS	91
CONDENSATE LINE IS PLUGGED	92
COMPRESSOR FAILS	92

SYSTEM FAILS TO TURN ON WHEN FIRST ACTIVATED IN SPRING/SUMMER	93
COMPRESSOR UNIT IS OUT OF LEVEL	93
EVAPORATIVE COOLER BLOWS WARM AIR	93
ELECTRICAL	94
LIGHTS FLICKER WHEN APPLIANCES ARE TURNED ON	94
BREAKERS TRIP OR FUSES BLOW FREQUENCY	94
ALUMINUM WIRE, NOT COPPER WIRE, WAS INSTALLED	95
LIGHT FIXTURES TARNISH	95
LIGHT SWITCHES AND OUTLET PLATES PROTRUDE TOO FAR FROM WALL	95
LIGHT SWITCHES STICK OR MUST BE JIGGLED TO TURN THE LIGHT ON	95
WALL OUTLET IN BEDROOM DOES NOT WORK	96
BATHROOM FANS / LAUNDRY FANS ARE NOISY	96
PLUMBING	96
WATER OR GAS PIPING LEAKS	96
WATER TASTES FUNNY, SMELLS, OR IS DISCOLORED	97
TOLIET BACKS UP, DRAINS BACK UP	98
INADEQUATE WATER PRESSURE	98
SEWER GAS SMELL COMING FROM DRAIN	98
COPPER WATER PIPES OR BLACK GAS PIPES ARE WET ON THE OUTSIDE	99
FAUCETS DRIP	99
SINK/TUB IS CHIPPED	99
SHOWER HEAD PIPE/TUB SPOUT IS LOOSE	100
FIBERGLASS TUB/SHOWER FLEXES WHEN OCCUPIED	100
WATER DRAINS FROM SINK/TUB WHEN STOPPED IS ENGAGED	100
BRASS BATHROOM FAUCETS AND DRAINS TARNISH	101
TOLIET RUNS CONTINUOUSLY	101
TOLIET LEAKS AT FLOOR	101
LACK OF HOT WATER	102
WATER HEATER IS NOT EARTHQUAKE SECURED, AS REQUIRED	102
ELECTRIC WATER HEATER CIRCUIT BREAKER TRIPS CONTINUOUSLY	103

FIRE SPRINKLER SYSTEM	103
FIRE SPRINKLER PIPES OR FITTINGS LEAK	103
SPRINKLER HEADS AND ESCUTCHEONS DO NOT FIT FLUSH TO WALL, OR ARE OUT OF LINE WITH DRYWALL OPENINGS	103
TELEPHONE	104
NO DIAL TONE, OR STATIC SOUNDS ARE HEARD	104
CABLE TV	104
TV RECEPTION IS SNOWY, WAVEY OR OTHERWISE UNCLEAR	104
GROUNDS	104
DRAINAGE	104
WATER DOES NOT DRAIN AWAY FROM FOUNDATION	104
IMPROPER SITE DRAINAGE (AREAS BEYOND 5 FEET OF THE PERIMETER OF THE FOUNDATION)	105
SETTLING OF SOILS AROUND THE FOUNDATION	105
SETTLING OF SOILS AT UTILITY TRENCHES	106
LANDSCAPING	106
IMPROPER SOILS PREPARATION	106
PLANTS DIE WITHIN THE WARRANTY PERIOD	106
WEED GROWTH IN LANDSCAPED AREAS	107
IRRIGATION	108
IMPROPER DESIGN AND/OR INSTALLATION OF IRRIGATION SYSTEM	108
CONTROLLER/CLOCK DOES NOT OPERATE	108
RETAINING WALLS	108
WALL LEAKS	108
CRACKS IN WALLS AND MORTAR JOINTS	109
WHITE CHALK-LIKE SUBSTANCE APPEARS ON THE FACE OF THE WALL	109
WALL IS OUT OF PLUMB	109
FENCING	110
WOOD POSTS, PICKETS OR PANELS ARE ROTTING	110
FENCING IS PREMATURELY WEATHERED OR RUSTED	110
WARPS, KNOTS AND CRACKS EXIST IN FENCE BOARDS	111
MISCELLANEOUS	111
ICE AND SNOW	111
ROOF SAFE OR FAILS UNDER SNOW LOAD	111
DOORS AND WINDOWS ARE BLOCKED WITH SNOW	111

ICE DAMS CAUSE EAVES TO LEAK	112
NOISE TRANSMISSION	112
SOUNDS CAN BE HEARD THROUGH WALLS AND FLOORS	112
MOLD AND MILDEW	113
MOLD AND MILDEW GROWTH WHERE LEAKS OCCUR	113
MOLD AND MILDEW GROWTH AROUND WINDOWS, DOORS, BASEBOARDS, BATHROOM SURFACES, ABSENT OF OBVIOUS LEAKS	113
MILDEW GROWTH ON SIDING, STUCCO AND OTHER EXTERIOR SURFACES	114
MILDEW OR MOLD GROWTH IN HEATING AND VENTILATION DUCT WORK	115
MOLD OR MILDEW GROWTH NEAR ENCLOSED PLUMPING PIPES	115
SEPTIC TANKS	115
SEWER SYSTEM / DRAINS NOT OPERATING PROPERLY	115
SEPTIC TANK EMITS FOUL ODOR	116
SMOKE DETECTORS	116
DIRECTORS SOUND DURING USE OF FIREPLACE / KITCHEN	116
DETECTORS DO NOT OPERATE WHEN TESTED	117
BIBLIOGRAPHY AND REFERENCES	118

FOUNDATIONS

SLAB ON GRADE

CONCRETE FOUNDATION IS CRACKED

Cracks that occur in slab-on-grade floors should not exceed 3/16-inch in width or 1/8-inch in vertical displacement over a 12-inch in length section. For slab floors that are to be covered with vinyl flooring or similar materials, cracks should not be visible in the finish floor at a distance of six feet under normal daylight conditions.

Resolution: Concrete cracks are inevitable, and the Builder cannot be held responsible for all concrete cracks. Builder should repair cracks that do not meet the acceptable guidelines. An acceptable fix is to fill the crack with a latex fortified cement mixture or epoxy.

Recommendation: Homeowner should be sure to maintain finished grade to ensure proper drainage away from foundation. Avoid overwatering. Install gutters and downspouts that are piped away from the foundation.

CONCRETE SLAB IS NOT LEVEL

The slab should be level and even, and any deviations should not exceed 1/2-inch of vertical change in 20 feet of length. This does not apply to multi-story building with post-tension concrete floors. Garage slabs are intentionally sloped away from inside walls towards the garage door to allow water to drain away from the structure.

Resolution: Determine the cause of the condition. If the condition is a result of improper construction and not a result of improper use or lack of maintenance by the Homeowner, then Builder should make necessary repairs.

CONCRETE SLAB IS UNEVEN

Concrete floors should not have areas of unevenness of more than 1/4-inch over a horizontal distance of 10 feet. This does not apply to multi-story buildings with post tension concrete floors.

Resolution: Builder is responsible to repair

GRADE BEAM AND PIER

EXTERIOR FOUNDATION GRADE BEAM IS OUT OF LEVEL

Over 40 feet of length, the top surface of the grade beam should be no more then 1-inch lower than the highest point, and no more then 1-inch higher than the lowest point. If the length of measurement is shorter, the allowable deviation is reduced proportionately.

Resolution: Builder shall furnish and install a level foundation for the house to be built upon. Adjust the foundation or mudsill to conform to proper guidelines.

FOUNDATION GRADE BEAM IS OUT OF SQUARE

If measuring the top of the grad beam: from the corner, measure one direction 12 feet. From the original starting point of the wall, measure 90 degrees the other direction 16 feet (12 feet and 16 feet from the corner should be at a 90 degree angle to one another). The diagonal distance should be within 1-inch in 20 feet.

Resolution: Builder should make proper adjustments to correct the out-of-square foundation – most likely in the framing.

EXPOSED WOOD AROUND PIERS OR GRADE BEAMS

The house should be completed with all wood or paper/cardboard removed from the **crawl space** and around the grade beam and piers. The only exception to this is cardboard that is wax treated and used to create a void under the grade beam as part of the construction process. Unless wood is **pressure treated** or foundation grade redwood, it cannot be placed within six inches of the ground.

Resolution: Builder should remove the materials.

Recommendation: Keep all wood or paper products from beneath the House/foundation. Avoid attaching anything wooded to the house if it makes contact with the earth. Do not store any wood or paper products in the crawl space.

EFFLORESCENSE (white powder) APPEARS ON CONCRETE SURFACES

Efflorescence on concrete surfaces is considered acceptable. This condition often occurs when one of the ingredients in the cement reacts with moist air.

Resolution: Homeowner can remove with water and a brush if considered unsightly.

BASEMENTS AND OTHER BELOW GRADE STRUCTURES

WATER TRICKLES INTO BASEMENT OF GARAGE THROUGH WALLS OR FLOOR

Water should not trickle or seep through basement or garage walls or floors

Resolution: Assuming that the finished grades have not been negatively altered, or that the installations of planter beds, flatwork, or irrigation have not altered the flow of water, and the Homeowner has not damaged any installed waterproofing systems, the Builder should make necessary repairs.

Recommendation: Homeowner should avoid making changes to surrounding grades that would cause rain or water to flow down the outside of the basement walls. This includes over-watering, construction planter beds without independent drainage, building "dams" between foundations and raised walkways and failure to keep swales and yard drains cleaned out. If basement dampness is an issue, the Homeowner should install a dehumidifier. In no event should the moisture barrier on the outside of the basement wall be damaged when planting or irrigation is installed

BASEMENT AND CONCRETE GARAGE WALLS ARE NOT PLUMB

Basement walls are considered out of plumb if they exceed more then 1-1/2-inch in 8 vertical feet

Resolution: Builder should take corrective action.

BASEMENT AND CONCRETE GARAGE WALLS ARE BOWED

Walls should not bow more then 1-inch in 8 feet (vertically or horizontally).

Resolution: Builder should take corrective action.

BASEMENT WALLS HAVE CRACKS OR HOLES, FLOORS HAVE CRACKS

Cracks in basement walls should not exceed 1/4-inch. Voids should not exceed 1-inch in diameter and 1-inch in depth. Cracks in basement floors should not exceed 1/4-inch in width and 3/16-inch in vertical displacement.

Resolution: Assuming cracks and voids do not leak, Builder should make repairs i.e. patching.

STANDING WATER IN CRAWL SPACE

Crawl spaces should be ventilated as required per Code, including cross ventilation and proper vent sizing, and graded so that there is no standing water covering more than 10% of the floor area at a depth of 1/2-inch. All grades outside the foundation walls should be away from the foundation at a minimum of 1/4-inch per foot. All downspouts should discharge away from the foundation onto splash blocks or be connected to solid drain lines.

Resolution: If standing water remains after 48 hour cessation of rain, Builder shall re-grade the crawl space to eliminate the standing water.

Recommendation: Be careful during the placement of concrete flatwork that the slope away from the foundation is not altered.

FLOORS AND CEILINGS

FLOOR SQUEAKS

Squeaks that are caused by loos sub-floors, i.e. plywood floor sheathing, loose nails or fasteners, may be considered unacceptable if the subject floor squeaks noticeably and continuously. NOTE: A squeak-proof floor cannot be guaranteed due to seasonal weather conditions that cause the frame to expand and contract.

Resolution: Floor squeaks that are a result of improperly installed floor joists, fasteners and/or sheathing, should be repaired by the Builder.

Recommendation: Floor squeaks are likely to occur with seasonal weather changes, and are usually a maintenance item.

WOOD SUBFLOORS OR CEILINGS ARE NOT FLAT

Any floor or ceiling that exceeds 1/4-inch depression or ridge in a 32-inch by 32-inch area should be considered non-performing.

Resolution: Builder should repair the subject area including any existing structure or finish material that may be destroyed and/or damaged because of the repair.

WOOD SUBFLOORS AND/OR DECKS ARE OUT OF LEVEL

No point on the surface of a wood subfloor or wood deck should be more then 1/2-inch higher or lower than any other point on that same surface within 20 feet.

Resolution: Builder should repair the non-performing area.

Recommendation: Do not store excessively heavy objects on a wood subfloor.

WOOD SUBFLOORS HAVE "SPRINGINESS" OR BOUNCE

All floors joists should meet the required size and rating as set forth in the applicable Building Code for the city or county in effect at the time the house was constructed. If manufactured floor trusses are used, the span and spacing should conform to the manufacturer's engineered calculations.

Resolution: If the floors are over-spanned for the grade of lumber permitted, the Builder should correct the deficiency.

SUBFLOOR IS OUT-OF-SQUARE

The diagonal of a triangle cannot be any greater or less than one-inch out of proportion of a triangle, with right angle legs of 12 feet and 16 feet. *Example: if a room measures 12 feet one direction and 16 feet in the other direction, a perfect diagonal measurement would be 20 feet. The length of the diagonal shall not be greater or less than one-inch within 20 feet.* Applying this to rooms of different sizes, the tolerance of the length of the third leg of the triangle (hypotenuse) cannot be more or less than 0.42% of its perfect diagonal length. An exception is an addition or remodel of an existing house, where the Builder and Homeowner agree that it is practical to match the existing out-of-square floor.

Resolution: If subfloors, or foundations, are far enough out of square that the frame members do not adequately bear on them, the foundation or frame should be repaired.

EXTERIOR WOOD BEAMS OR POSTS ARE WARPED, CRACKED OR SPLIT

Exposed wood beams or posts that have splits that exceed 1/2-inch in width and 6-inches in length are considered excessive and are unacceptable.

Resolution: Builder should repair or replace posts or beams.

Recommendation: Homeowner should conduct an annual inspection of exterior wood materials. Repairs within tolerance can be filled with wood filler. Significant dry-rot should be evaluated by a structural specialist.

WOOD BEAMS OR POSTS ARE TWISTED OR CUPPED

Any beam or post that twists more then 3/4-inch in an 8 foot section is considered unacceptable. Cups that exceed 1/2-inch in 12-inches of beam height are considered unacceptable.

Resolution: Builder should repair or replace deficient wood members.

Recommendation: All exterior wood should be inspected annually for any caulking separation or paint peeling and should be repaired immediately in order to prevent future problems.

WALLS

STUCCO WALLS

CRACKS ON STUCCO WALLS

All exterior stucco covered walls, soffits and/or garden walls should not have any cracks that exceed 1/8-inch in width or 1/8-inch in adjacent surface displacement. However, cracks less than 1/8-inch covering more than 33% of a one foot square area of a <u>dry</u> surface wall (similar to a spider web pattern), are unacceptable. If the wall is wet, it will show a disproportionate number of surface irregularities and cracks; this applies to walls measured when dry.

Resolution: The Builder has a duty to furnish a house that is free from excessive cracking.

Recommendation: Do not alter the finished grades around the perimeter of the foundation. Undrained, wet soil can cause foundation movement, which could result in stucco cracking. Expect some normal cracking in stucco.

WATER STAINS OR WATER DAMAGE TO INTERIOR WALLS

All lath and plaster should be installed in such a manner that will ensure the house to be watertight and free from any exterior water intrusion.

Resolution: Builder should determine the exact cause and make repairs as necessary.

Recommendation: If the house has wood trim around the windows and exterior doors, this trim should be inspected for gaps and caulked annually. If a leak appears, the Builder should be notified immediately.

COLOR COAT REPAIR WORK DOES NOT MATCH EXISTING COLOR

A poor color match is defined as a visible patch or area that can be seen by a layperson at a distance of 6 feet in indirect light. Any repair work that is necessary should be recolored from one corner to the other corner at full height, or properly "fogged" to acceptably blend the color coats.

Resolution: Builder should match the existing color as close as possible and should complete the repairs by recoloring the entire wall and/or line of sight that needs repair.

WEEP SCREED FLASHING IS RUSTING OR RUST MARKS APPEAR ON NUMBEROUS PLACES ON THE SURFACE OF THE OUTSIDE WALLS

Weep screeds should not become rusted to the point of deterioration. Rust marks on the surface of walls are considered unacceptable, if more than 5 marks measuring over 1-inch long occur per 100 square feet.

Resolution: If the weep screed becomes deteriorated to the point that it has rusted and no longer serves the purpose for which it was intended, the Builder should remove and replace it as necessary. Builder should seal the rusted areas and recolor the wall.

Recommendation: Keep irrigation water from spraying against the stucco. Do not allow vegetation to overgrow in the screed area.

STUCCO COLOR COAT IS SEPARATING FROM THE BROWN COAT

Stucco color should not separate from the brown coat.

Resolution: Builder should make appropriate repairs.

WET SPOTS REMAIN ON STUCCO WALLS AFTER A RAIN STORM

This condition is normal and acceptable.

Resolution: None.

LATH IS VISIBLE THROUGH THE STUCCO

Lath should not be visible through stucco, nor should any portion of the lath protrude through stucco.

Resolution: Builder should make necessary repairs.

FOAM BOARD IS VISIBLE THROUGH THE STUCCO

Foam boards should not be visible at any surface area of the one-coat system. All foam boards should be covered by at least 3/8-inch of base and finish coat.

Resolution: Builder should make necessary repairs.

WHITE POWDERY SUBSTANCE (EFFLORESCENCE) APPEARS ON STUCCO WALLS IN WINTER MONTHS

The white powdery substance (known as efflorescence) that appears on stucco walls and bare concrete slabs during the rainy season are caused by lime in the cement reacting with moist air. It is considered acceptable and can easily be removed with water and a brush.

Resolution: Homeowner maintenance

WOOD TRIM IS EMBEDDED IN STUCCO

Wood embedded in stucco is considered acceptable. Water resistant building paper must run continuously behind the embedded wood to prevent moisture from entering the wall cavity. Wood will shrink as it dries our (especially large beams) and a gap may develop between the wood and the stucco. If the gap exceeds 1/4-inch at any part or warps more than 1/4-inch away from the face of the building, it is considered unacceptable.

Resolution: Builder should repair or replace excessively gapped or warped wood trim.

Recommendation: It is very important for homeowners to inspect for gaps and caulk around all wood members with at least a 25-year rated caulk before the rainy season begins. Any old caulking should be completely removed before re-caulking the area.

STUCCO WALL APPEARS "WAVY" DURING SUNSET HOURS OR WHEN LIGHTED WITH LANDSCAPE LIGHTS

Stucco walls that exhibit a wavy characteristic under low light or artificial light are acceptable.

Resolution: None

PLYWOOD BEHIND STUCCO IS DELAMINATING OR SPLITTING

Any sub-surface plywood, i.e. plywood that is installed behind wood siding or stucco, that warps or splits excessively is unacceptable and should be replaced. "Excessive" means that the laminations can be easily separated using a hammer's claw.

Resolution: Builder should locate and seal the source of water intrusion, as well as repair and/or replace any plywood that does not conform. Any finishes that have been damaged and/or removed will need to be replaced as necessary.

Recommendation: Homeowner should conduct periodic scheduled maintenance, i.e. caulking and painting as necessary to prevent potential problems.

EXTERIOR TRIM

THERE ARE GAPS BETWEEN THE HOUSE BODY AND THE EXTERIOR TRIM

Within the first year, or longer if the warranty states, there shall be no gap larger than 3/8-inch between any trim piece and the house siding or stucco, or 1/4-inch between butt joints or miter joints of the trim pieces themselves. Water shall not be allowed to intrude into any part of the wall cavity or column system.

Resolution: Within the warranty period, the Builder shall correct any gaps in wood trim that are in excess of 3/8-inch. Caulking is acceptable unless the gap is greater than 3/8-inch. For gaps greater than 3.8-inch, the trim piece should be replaced.

EXTERIOR TRIM BOARD IS SPLIT, BOWED, TWISTED, OR CUPPED

Splits wider than 3/8-inch in three inches of length are non-performing. Bows and twists in excess of 3/8-inches in six feet of length are non-performing. Cups that exceed 3/16-inch in four inches of width are non-performing.

Recommendation: Homeowner does not have any responsibility within the warranty period, but is responsible for maintenance of the trim form the end of the warranty period.

HARDBOARD SIDING

EXTERIOR SURFACE IS BUCKLED

Hardboard siding should not warp or buckle more than 3/16-inch out of plane when nailed to studs placed at 16 inches on center

Resolution: Builder shall replace at time of construction if deficient.

Recommendation: Homeowner is responsible for maintain the siding system in a sound, water-resisting condition. Among other things this involves painting the siding on a regular schedule, re-caulking joints periodically, and making sure that exposure to earth, paved surfaces, and water are properly controlled.

DRIP EDGE OF LAP SIDING IS SWOLLEN OR SPLIT

Swelling should not exceed approximately 10% of the original thickness of the drip edge, causing the material to crack and separate.

Resolution: Builder should paint siding systems in accordance with the material and workmanship requirements published by the manufacturer, paying special attention to the complete coating of all drip edges. Drip edges that have deteriorated due to abuse or lack of homeowner maintenance are not the responsibility of the Builder.

Recommendation: It is important to observe the condition of painted siding surfaces on a periodic basis. An annual inspection is recommended. When paints begin to show signs of wear, this often first occurs in limited areas. Undertaking maintenance ant touch up painting before paint degradation proceeds too far will significantly extend the life of the siding system. Homeowner should also prevent irrigation heads from spraying onto siding

SIDING MATERIAL IS SWOLLEN OR SPLIT AROUND NAILS

Siding should not visibly swell around nails. The usual pattern of unacceptable swelling is a "donut" shaped thickening of the siding material around the nail head. Nails should not be driven deeper than the surface of the siding.

Resolution: Builder should ensure that nails are not overset, and the proper types of nails (as recommended by the siding manufacturer) are used in the installation of siding. If nails are not driven more than halfway through the siding, caulking and painting is an acceptable repair. If the nail is driven into more than half the thickness of the siding, another nail must be properly driven in an adjacent location, and the original nail should be caulked and painted.

Recommendation: Maintenance of siding surfaces, including painting on an appropriate schedule, will significantly extend the life of the siding and limit the tendency to swell around nails

SIDING SPLITS, SOFTENS, AND ROTS AT THE BASE OF WALLS

Siding should not split, soften or rot.

Resolution: Builder should not permit the construction of any condition that will result in siding deterioration at the base of walls. If such a condition exists, the Builder should make the necessary repairs.

Recommendation: Homeowner must guard against introducing conditions that could result in deterioration of siding. For example, the Homeowner must maintain appropriate clearances between siding and earth or paving. When landscape improvements are installed, care should be taken to maintain the original clearance. The homeowner is also responsible for proper maintenance of systems that can adversely affect siding. Another example: changes in sprinkler head spray patterns that cause irrigation water to spray directly onto siding must be avoided.

BUTT JOINTS ARE TOO WIDE

Butt joints (the gaps at the end of the board) should not be wider than 3/16-inch.

Resolution: Butt joints that do not conform shall be brought into conformance by the Builder.

SIDING IS CROOKED

Siding boards should be within 1/4-inch of level over 10 feet of length

Resolution: Builder shall reinstall non-conforming boards.

SIDING IS SOFT AND ROTTING AT WINDOW AND DOOR TRIM, RAILINGS, AND OTHER LOCATIONS

Siding should not be soft, rot, or deteriorate. Joints between adjacent pieces of siding, siding and trim, siding and rail caps, and other such components, should be assembled in such a way that siding deterioration resulting from water intrusion does not occur.

Resolution: Builder should install siding-to-siding and siding-to-trim joints in a sound, waterproof manner that readily sheds water. Non-performing conditions from improper construction should be repaired.

Recommendation: Homeowner is responsible for periodic maintenance of such items as caulked joints that are essential barriers to unwanted water entry into the siding system.

SIDING HAS RAISED NAIL HEADS

Nails should be set with the bottom of the nail head flush with the surface of the siding. Use only nails recommended by the siding manufacturer. **Resolution:** Builder should ensure that nailing is performed in accordance with the requirements of the manufacturer. Nails that protrude at the outset of installation are a result of poor nailing techniques. Nails that protrude progressively over time may be the result of using the wrong types of nails, or installation into framing lumber with high moisture content.

PANEL SIDING

JOINTS AT PANEL EDGES ARE EXCESSIVELY WIDE OR RAISED

Joints at panel edges should not exceed 3/16-inch in width or 3/16-inch in a plane from the adjacent panel.

Resolution: Builder should repair or replace any non-conforming panels.

PANELS ARE DELAMINATING

Siding panels should not delaminate.

Resolution: Builder should repair or replace any non-conforming panels.

PANELS ARE BOWED

Panel bows in excess of 1/4-inch between studs at 16-omcjes on center are unacceptable.

Resolution: Builder should adjust the building frame or the individual panel.

VINYL SIDING

VINYL SIDING IS BOWED

Bows in vinyl siding should not exceed 1/4-inch between **studs** placed at 16 inches on center.
Resolution: Builder should make repairs as necessary to conform to the guidelines.

VINYL SIDING IS FADED OR BLOTCHED

Over a period of years, most vinyl siding will fade uniformly. Non-uniform fading (or blotching) is an unacceptable condition and is considered non-performing. Most vinyl siding manufacturers warrant their product against fading and non-uniform discoloration.

Resolution: If the vinyl siding condition does not meet the manufacturer's warranty standard, the Builder should assist the Homeowner in dealing with the manufacturer for repair or replacement of the non-conforming siding.

Recommendation: Refer to the manufacturer's warranty on vinyl siding.

CEMENT BOARD SIDING

CEMENT BOARD SIDING IS CRACKED OR CHIPPED

Any cracks in cement board siding less than 2 inches in length or 1/8-inch in width are considered acceptable; Cracks in excess are unacceptable. Chips or full breaks in excess of 1/2-inch in radius are unacceptable.

Resolution: Cracks or chips that measure within the guidelines should be caulked and painted. Cracks or chips that exceed the standard should be replaced.

GENERAL SIDING

NAILS HAVE STAINED SIDING

Stains that "bleed" into the siding for more than 1/2-inch in length as viewed from a distance of 20 feet under normal daylight conditions are unacceptable.

Resolution: Builder should make repairs as necessary if the conditions are a result of improper installation.

Recommendation: Siding nails should be inspected annually. Bleeds can be sealed with a clear aerosol sealer. An exterior painting schedule should follow to ensure proper maintenance.

INTERIOR WALLS

WALLS ARE OUT OF PLUMB

Walls are considered out of plumb if they are more then 3/8-inch in any 32 inches of vertical measurement, or they exceed 1/2-inch in 8 foot cumulative vertical measurement. An exception is an addition or remodel of an existing house, where the Builder and Homeowner agree that it is practical to match the existing out-of-plumb wall (provided that the out-of-plumb wall does not pose a structural threat).

Resolution: Builder makes the necessary repairs

WALLS ARE BOWED

All interior and exterior walls have different finishes, however the allowable tolerance for "rough framed walls" that are bowed should not be greater than 1/4-inch in a 32 inch horizontal or vertical measurement, not to exceed 1/2-inch in 8 feet of length or height.

Resolution: Builder shall repair any wall that does not meet guidelines. All finishes should be replaced as necessary to complete said repairs.

INTERIOR WALL INTERSECTIONS ARE NOT PERPENDICULAR ON WALLS THAT ARE DESIGNED TO MEET AT 90 DEGREE ANGLES

The tolerance for an out of perpendicular condition where walls intersect shall be 1/4-inch for the first 10 feet of length; thereafter, the rate of deviation shall not exceed 1/2-inch in 20 meet of more of wall length.

Resolution: Builder shall either move the wall or furr out the wall

SHEAR WALLS

SHEAR WALLS ARE INADEQUATE

The structural integrity of any shear wall cannot fall below the values set forth in the applicable Building Code.

Resolution: If the Builder believes that the wall has been designed in excess of Code requirements, the Builder may obtain the opinion of a licensed structural engineer that the wall in its present condition meets the requirements of the Building Code

SHEAR WALLS OR HOLD DOWNS ARE MISSING

Shear walls and hold downs that are shown on the structural drawings approved by the local governing agency that issues the building permit must be installed as shown.

Resolution: Builder shall retrofit a hold down as allowed by the local governing agency and/or provide an alternate plan of repair from a licensed structural engineer.

ROOFS

FLASHING

FLASHING HAS RUSTED

Sheet metal flashing should not rust during the warranty period.

Resolution: Builder shall replace or repaint sheet metal flashings that have rusted within the warranty period.

Recommendation: After the warranty period, homeowner should scrape sheet metal free of any sign of rust and repaint.

FLASHING IS NOT SET TIGHT TO THE SHINGLES OR TILE

Sheet metal flashings should be no more than 1/4-inch above the highest plane of the material that it is intended to cover.

Resolution: Builder shall make adjustments to correct deficiency

STRUCTURAL COMPONENTS

ROOF RIDGE SAGS

Roof ridge deflection should not exceed 2-inches in 16 feet of length

Resolution: Builder should repair any condition caused during original construction.

Recommendation: Homeowner should not install and/or fasten any products and/or materials on the roof. The installation of materials and/or products by the homeowner may void any warranty work by the Builder. The homeowner should contact and/or consult with the Builder prior to the installation of any "add-on" products. The Builder will assume no responsibility for the roof systems when the homeowner installs anything on the floor of makes any modifications whatsoever without approval of the Builder.

ROOF SHEATHING IS BOWED

Roof sheathing should have a maximum deflection of 3/8-inch up or down in 2 feet of length. Roof sheathing should conform to the recommendations of the roofing material manufacturer, as well as the specification of the building designer and the minimum requirements of the Building Code.

Resolution: Builder should make the required repairs.

SLATE, CONCRETE AND CLAY TILES

ROOF LEAKS

All roof systems should be installed in a watertight fashion and should not allow any kind of water intrusion under <u>normal</u> inclement weather conditions; "normal" means what is typical for that particular geographic region.

Resolution: If the roof leaks under normal weather conditions, the Builder should correct any verified roof or flashing leaks, as well as repair any damages that are a result of the subject leak. The Builder assumes no responsibility for leaks caused by extreme weather conditions or by homeowner negligence.

Recommendation: The homeowner is responsible for periodic maintenance, i.e. cleaning of all roof drains, gutters and downspouts of leaves and other foreign debris and for checking all areas that have a caulking or sealant type material such as vents, pipes penetrations, and sheet metal flashings for cracked sealant, etc.

LOOSE OR FALLING ROOF TILES OR SLATE

Tiles should not be loose or fall from the roof. They should be fastened in accordance with the manufacturer's published attachment schedule.

Resolution: Builder should remove and/or refasten any non-conforming tiles caused during original installation.

Recommendation: Homeowner should conduct periodic inspections along all roof-to-wall intersections and look for loose or slipping tiles. Any work or inspection that requires access to the roof should be conducted by a qualified roofing specialist.

CHIPPED OR BROKEN ROOF TILES OR SLATE

All cracked and broken tiles are considered unacceptable, if installed in that condition. Chips smaller then 3/4-inch are acceptable, providing that the total number of chipped tiles does not exceed more than 10 percent of the square footage of the plane (face) of the roof. Tile with chipped edges that are placed under sheet metal flashing are considered acceptable.

Resolution: Builder should replace any missing, broken, cracked or excessively chipped tiles which are a result of the Builder's work.

Recommendation: Homeowner should inspect the roof for any cracked and/or broken tiles within the first month of occupancy. Homeowners should not walk on the roof, make any roof penetrations, or fasten any objects to the roof. If the Homeowner cannot inspect the roof with a ladder, or by observation from a safe higher vantage point, it is strongly advised that the Homeowner hire a qualified roofing inspector to perform the job.

IMPROPER EXPOSURE, LAPPING AND SPACING OF TILES OR SLATE

Exposure should not exceed that of the manufacturer's installation recommendations, or that of the Building Code.

Resolution: The Builder should repair any tiles that have exposed nails. The exception is the **rake** tiles along the edge of the roof, which often have exposed nails.

LACK OF ADEQUATE NAILING

All roof tiles should be fastened according to the manufacturer's recommendations as well as with the Building Code.

Resolution: The Builder should make the appropriate repairs to make sure roof tiles are adequately nailed.

MISSING OR IMPROPERLY APPLIED SHEET METAL FLASHINGS

Roof flashing should not leak under normal conditions. The Builder is not responsible for this condition when the causes of leaks are a result of ice build-up, snow, wind driven rain or homeowner negligence.

Resolution: Builder will repair any flashing deficiencies resulting from improper installation.

Recommendation: Homeowners are responsible for keeping all sheet metal valleys, gutters, and downspouts free from ice build-up, snow, leaves, and/or other foreign debris.

EFFLORESCENCE (Appearance of light colored deposits on concrete tiles)

Concrete roof tiles should be uniform in color and free from extensive efflorescence. Minor efflorescence is considered normal and acceptable.

Resolution: None

COMPOSITION ASPHALT SHINGLES

ROOF LEAKS

All roof systems should, at the time of installation, be watertight and free from any kind of water intrusion under normal inclement weather conditions; "normal" meaning what is typical for that particular geographic region

Resolution: If the roof leaks under normal weather conditions, the Builder should correct any verified roof or flashing leaks, and repair damages that are results of the subject leak. The builder will not be responsible for leaks caused by homeowner negligence, such as improper fastening to, installations on, or penetrations of the roof.

Recommendation: Homeowner is responsible for annual maintenance, i.e. cleaning of all roof drains, valleys, chimney crickets, gutters and downspouts of leaves and/or foreign debris; checking areas that have a sealant type material, i.e. vents, pipe penetrations, and inspecting all sheet metal flashing for deteriorated sealant, etc. Homeowners should also avoid installing products and/or fastening items to or through the roof.

SHINGLES HAVE BLOWN OFF

Shingles should not suffer damages under normal wind loads for a particular geographic region, as set forth in wind design guidelines.

Resolution: If shingles are damaged by wind, and wind loads are within the wind design standards of the manufacturer, the Builder should make all the necessary repairs. Builder is not responsible for conditions caused by homeowner misuse or improper maintenance.

SHINGLES ARE NOT HORIZONTALLY ALIGNED

Unless the Builder is trying to achieve a special architectural effect by staggering the ends or rows of the shingles, shingles should be reasonably straight with even courses.

Resolution: If courses are over exposed or underexposed from the manufacturer's installation recommendations, the Builder should make all the repairs that are necessary to meet the installation recommendations.

SHINGLES ARE CURLED OR CUPPED AT EDGES AND CORNERS

Asphalt shingle edges and corners need not be flat, but they should not curl or cup in excess of 1/2-inch. Fastener heads should not be exposed. However, the appearance of shingles should be within manufacturer's standards or specifications.

Resolution: If the curling and cupping becomes widespread and is not within the manufacturer's specifications, the Builder should replace shingles as necessary to meet the manufacturer's standards.

Recommendation: As roofs age, particular attention should be paid to the condition of curled and cupped shingles. An occasional "tune-up" by a licensed and qualified roofing contractor can extend the life of the roof significantly.

SHINGLES OVERHANG EDGES OF ROOF, TOO FAR OR TOO LITTLE

Composition shingles should overhang the roof edges no less than 1/4-inch, and not more than 3/4-inch unless the manufacturer's standards and specifications indicate otherwise.

Resolution: The Builder should replace as necessary

ASPHALT SHINGLES HAVE DEVELOPED SURFACE BUCKLING

Buckling that exceeds 3/8-inch in height is considered unacceptable

Resolution: Builder needs to make necessary repairs if buckling exceeds guidelines.

SHADING OR SHADOWING PATTERN APPEARS ON THE SHINGLES

Shading or shadowing is considered acceptable.

Resolution: None

EROSION OF SHINGLE SURFACING MATERIALS

At the time of installation, mineral granules should remain adhered to the surface of the shingles and no bare spots should be observable when looking down at the roof.

Resolution: Builder should provide adequate protection to finished roof surfaces during subsequent building component construction (e.g. masonry, siding, etc.) to prevent undue abrasion of mineral granules. Builder should refer occurrences of significant mineral granule loss to the manufacturer, as this is likely a manufacturing defect.

Recommendation: Homeowner should not permit excessive access to the roof and when access is required, adequate protection should be provided to the roof surface to prevent loss of mineral granules.

UNSEALED SHINGLE TABS

Shingles or shingle tabs should be adhered to underlying shingles.

Resolution: The Builder should fasten shingles in conformance to recommendations published by the shingle manufacturer, and/or standards published by recognized industry associations. Non-performing installations should be corrected.

ROOF VENTILATION

ATTIC VENT OR LOUVER LEAKS

Vents and louvers should not leak under normal weather conditions for the geographic region. Some leakage during extreme weather conditions may occur and is acceptable.

Resolution: Builder should make repairs that are necessary to eliminate any water intrusion during normal weather conditions. If water intrusion occurs between the vent and the wall finish and is a result of improper installation, the Builder should make the necessary repairs to eliminate leakage

Recommendation: Keep all vents and louvers free from any obstructions. Do not allow birds to nest in vents.

EAVES

LEAKES OR STAINS APPEAR AT THE UNDERSIDE OF THE EAVES

The roof should be installed in a watertight condition.

Resolution: If the roof eave leaks during normal regional weather and the leaks are a result of improper installation, the Builder should conduct repairs as necessary.

Recommendation: Homeowner is responsible for providing proper maintenance, including keeping gutters free from debris, clearing ice dams that may develop, etc.

ROOF SAGS OR BOWS AT EAVES AND FASCIA

Deviation from flatness (a horizontal line) at eves or fascia board should be no greater than 1/2-inch in any 8 feet of length.

Resolution: Builder should correct sags or bows not in accordance with guidelines.

BUILT-UP ROOFING AND OTHER LOW SLOPE ROOFS

STANDING WATER ON ROOF

Minor ponding is acceptable, providing that it does not exceed 1/2-inch in depth, and is dry within 48 hours after cessation of rainfall.

Resolution: Builder is responsible for providing drainage with a positive slope for the finished roof. A flat roof should have a minimum slope of 1/4-inch of drop to the edge or drain for each 12-inches across the roof surface.

Recommendation: This type of roof system needs a bi-annual inspection and maintenance program, i.e., clearing any debris that may damage the roof membrane, sealing any cracks, tears or rips, and keeping drains, gutters and downspouts free from debris. Also, where the roof turns up to a wall or skylight, the felt material is susceptible to deterioration and my produce leaks if not properly maintained. If the roof has parapet walls, then all overflow scuppers or primary and secondary drains must be kept free of leaves, gravel, and debris

ROOF LEAKS

The roof should not leak under weather conditions that are considered normal for the geographic area.

Resolution: Builder should install a watertight roof. If the roof leaks during normal weather, the Builder should repair the deficiency.

Recommendation: After-market products such as deck boards, satellite dishes and solar panels should not be fastened directly to the roof systems without consulting the original Builder or a licensed roofing contractor. Homeowner should be aware that fastening a product to the roof system could cause the warranty to be voided. Minimize the amount of walking that is done on the roof. Homeowner should also schedule a routine maintenance program.

ROOF MEMBRANE HAS BUBBLES OR BLISTERS

Bubbles or blisters that exceed 12-inches in diameter are unacceptable. Small and unbroken bubbles/blisters that are less than 12-inches in diameter are considered acceptable. Bubbles or blisters that cover more than 20% of the roof are unacceptable.

Resolution: Builder should make any necessary repairs that do not conform.

Recommendation: As the roof starts to age, homeowners will need to provide periodic maintenance to joints and separations. Areas that have received tar or caulking type materials will also need periodic maintenance due to age and structure movement. Homeowner should pay particular attention to locations where dissimilar materials meet (i.e., plumbing vents or metal flashing). The joining of dissimilar materials is a prime location for water intrusion, especially as tar and caulking become more brittle and crack.

ROOF MEMBRANE HAS SPLITS OR TEARS

Splitting and tearing of the roof membrane are unacceptable.

Resolution: Builder should make repairs if condition is not a result of homeowner negligence.

Recommendation: A maintenance schedule should be started as soon as the house is occupied. As the roof ages, maintenance becomes increasingly important. The homeowner will need to provide maintenance to asphalt cements, joints, and separations. Homeowner should pay particular attention to where the roof ties into dissimilar materials. The tie-in of dissimilar materials (materials that are not of the same kind, i.e. wood in contact with steel, stucco in contact with wood, etc.) are prime locations for water intrusion, especially over time, as roofing compounds like asphalt cement and caulking can crack, separate and become brittle.

ROOF HAS BARE SPOTS

An even layer of gravel or mineral should be firmly embedded into the flood coat, with no bare spots showing. Where the membrane turns up on vertical projections (such as parapet walls, skylights, and plumbing vents), flashing or granular surfacing suitable for exposure should be used to protect membranes.

Resolution: The Builder should furnish a roof that is fully coated or surface with gravel or mineral and roofing compounds (if the roof is a surface gravel system). If at the time of installation, the roof does not meet the guidelines, the Builder should make appropriate repairs. The Builder is not responsible if bare spots have been created by extreme wind conditions or if the condition is caused by improper homeowner usage or lack of maintenance.

Recommendation: Homeowner has the responsibility of keeping the roof, roof drains, gutters and downspouts free of any foreign debris. Gravel or mineral has a tendency to clog drains and fill gutters. Always make plans to check the roof prior to and after any inclement weather and/or winter rains.

ROOFING MATERIAL AT THE ROOF-TO-WALL INTERSECTION IS SPLITTING

Splits, tears or rips are not acceptable.

Resolution: If the roof leaks are a result of poor or inadequate flashing, counter-flashing and/or the lack of adequate cant strips, and the leak is not the result of homeowner negligence, the Builder should make necessary repairs.

Recommendation: Avoid walking on the roof. Avoid stepping or walking on locations where materials transition from horizontal to vertical.

UNSEALED LAPS

All laps of the roof membrane should be properly sealed.

Resolution: Builder should install the roof membrane with all laps properly sealed.

FASTENER BACK-OUT

All fasteners should be properly sized and installed, per manufacturer's instructions.

Resolution: Builder should install the roof system with all fasteners properly sized and securely installed per manufacturer's specifications. Fasteners found to be backing out within the accepted warranty period should be replaced.

Recommendation: Homeowner should retain a qualified roofing professional to perform annual inspections of the roof, noting and repairing any irregularities that are found, such as backed out fasteners.

ACCUMULATION OF BROWN RESIDUE FROM ASPHALT ROOFING PRODUCTS

This is an acceptable and normal condition

Resolution: None

EXTERIOR COMPONENTS

WALKWAYS AND DRIVEWAYS

DRIVEWAY IS CRACKED

Any crack that exceeds 1/4-inch in width or exceeds 1/4-inch in vertical displacement is considered unacceptable. Minor cracking is normal. A crack that occurs along a joint that is cut into the driveway when it was poured is considered acceptable, provided the crack does not exceed 3/4-inch in width. Further, this guideline includes spacing control joints in the wet concrete at industry recommended intervals based upon the thickness of the slab. A nominal 4-inch thick slab should have control joints spaced at 12 feet or less.

Resolution: Builder should meet the above guideline, providing the cracking is not a result of any homeowner misuse or negligence (this includes homeowner overwatering of the surrounding area and causing the soils to expand). If the concrete cracking exceeds the guidelines, Builder should make the appropriate repairs as needed. Builder shall also be responsible for the replacement of any landscape that was damaged as a result of the repairs.

Recommendation: Cracks that occur at control joints are to be maintained by the homeowner. This maintenance consists of filling the crack with a suitable concrete caulk. Homeowner should also maintain the area around the driveway in a way that will not allow soils to be washed away from beneath the driveway. Tree roots are a primary cause for concrete to heave and/or crack in landscaped areas. When placing trees in the vicinity of any concrete product, it is important to consider the potential growth of the root system (for example, palm trees have very small root balls, while the root system of a willow is extensive and will cause significant heaving of drives and walks). Homeowner should seek the advice of a licensed landscape architect or contractor and install a root barrier system in these instances.
WALKWAY IS CRACKED

Any crack that exceeds 1/4-inch in width or exceeds 1/4-inch in vertical displacement is considered unacceptable. Cracking that occurs at a control joint is acceptable, unless the crack exceeds 1-inch in width and 1/4-inch in vertical displacement. Minor cracking is considered normal.

Resolution: Builder should make repairs as long as the deficiency is not caused by homeowner negligence. Builder is also responsible for the replacement of any landscape material that was damaged as a result of the repairs.

Recommendation: Cracks that occur at control joints are to be maintained by the homeowner. Homeowner should also maintain the area around the sidewalks in a way that will not allow soils to be washed away from beneath them. Tree roots generally pose the biggest threat to concrete sidewalks. When homeowners decide that they want to install a tree, they often make their decision solely on the beauty of the tree. However, when placing trees in the vicinity of any concrete product, the most important consideration should be the potential for growth of the root system.

WATER PONDS ON SIDEWALK

Any standing or ponding water that exceeds 3/8-inch in depth in a circle more than one foot in diameter is considered unacceptable. All water should drain off or evaporate within 24 hours of cessation of rain.

Resolution: Builder should make necessary repairs provided the unacceptable condition was not cause by actions of the homeowner. Builder should repair any landscape that is damaged as a result of the repairs.

Recommendation: Homeowner should not let any irrigation undermine the sidewalks. Sidewalks need to have a very solid foundation in order to prevent any cracking or damage from occurring.

CONCRETE DRIVEWAY THAT ABUTS THE GARAGE IS HIGHER THAN THE GARAGE SLAB

A concrete driveway should never be higher than the interior portion of the garage slab that abuts. A deviation in two adjoin sections of concrete should not be greater than 1/2-inch between the two adjoining surfaces.

Resolution: Builder should make necessary repairs.

DRIVEWAY APPROACH IS TOO STEEP, CAUSING VEHICLES TO SCRAP OR TO BOTTOM OUT

Driveway approach should meet the standards of the local municipality at the time of construction.

Resolution: Builder does not have a responsibility to make driveway approaches suitable for all vehicles. If driveway approach does not meet the local municipality's standard, the Builder should make the necessary repairs.

CONCRETE DRIVEWAY IS SPALLING, SCALING OR CHIPPING

The surface of the concrete should not disintegrate to the point that the aggregate (small rocks) are showing in more than 5% of the driveway surface area.

Resolution: Builder should make necessary repairs if surface spalls, scales or chips exceed the guideline, as long as the deficiency is not related to homeowner negligence.

Recommendation: Homeowner should not spill acidic products or create excessive landscape moisture that may cause damage to the concrete surface. Homeowner assumes the risk of damage to concrete (and surrounding landscape areas) by using rock salt as an ice-removing agent.

CONCRETE STOOP IS PULLING AWAY FROM THE FOUNDATION

Concrete stoops that join to the foundation should not separate form the foundation by more than 1/4-inch.

Resolution: If the steps or stoops are separated from 1/4-inch to one-inch, the Builder may fill the separation or replace the stoop at his option. Stoops that are separated by gaps in excess of one-inch should be repaired or replaced as appropriate.

Recommendation: Separations up to 1/4-inch are the responsibility of the homeowner to maintain. Concrete caulk may be used to fill the gap.

GARAGE DOORS

GARAGE DOOR LEAKS WATER/SNOW AT HEAD, JAMBS OR THRESHOLD

Install garage doors in accordance with the recommendations of the manufacturer. Some water or snow can be expected to enter around the door under high wind conditions. This is acceptable. The garage slab should slope toward the door at 3-inches per 20 feet. The driveway surface at the garage door should be sloped to inhibit the entrance of water. There should also be a vertical drop of up to 1/2-inch between the driveway slab and the garage slab, so as to act as a weather break. If the garage is located at the bottom of a down sloped driveway, the two feet of driveway closet to the garage slab should be sloped away from the garage slab at a rate of 1/4-inch per foot. A drain that runs parallel to the garage door is also acceptable.

Resolution: Builder should adjust door in the event that excessive water entry occurs at jambs and head. Garage door weather stripping can be very effective.

GARAGE DOOR FAILS TO OPERATE PROPERLY OR GETS JAMMED

Barring damage caused by homeowner misuse, garage doors should operate smoothly and completely, as intended by the manufacturer.

Resolution: Unless the homeowner has been negligent or abusive in the use of the garage doors, the Builder should make the appropriate adjustments to malfunctioning doors.

Recommendation: Homeowner should maintain garage doors in accordance with the manufacturer's recommendations and avoid abusive or negligent use of doors that could result in damage. It is the homeowner's responsibility to keep the metal rods that span the top and bottom of the door in a tight condition and in proper alignment.

GARAGE DOOR "MYSTERIOUSLY" OPENS

Garage door openers should operate only on their own assigned frequencies. Random external signals should not cause the door to open or close.

Recommendation: Read the instruction manual that is furnished with the automatic door opener and change the opener code.

DECKS AND PATIOS

WATER PONDS ON DECKS AND PATIOS

There should be no more than 3/8-inch of water standing in a ponded area 24 hours after cessation of rain.

Resolution: Assuming the condition is a result of original construction; repair the surface of the deck or patio to create the proper slope, i.e. 1/4-inch to the foot.

Recommendation: Keep decks clean and free of dirt and debris so that they will not become slippery or plug the deck drains during storms. If deck drains are installed, they should be flushed with a garden hose prior to the start of the rainy season and periodically during the rainy season. Overflow drains should be inspected to ensure that they are not clogged with leaves or other debris. Potted plants should not be placed directly on the deck surface. They should be placed on stands or spacers to allow air to circulate underneath. Plant stands with metal legs should be avoided or protected the deck surface from penetration by the metal legs.

DECK MEMBERS ARE ROTTING

Exposed deck structural members such as posts, beams, and joists should be pressure treated wood, or Code approved wood that is naturally resistant to decay. Other wood, such as Douglas fir, or southern pine may be used if it is wrapped with an approved building paper as part of the stucco or siding cladding process.

Resolution: Construct structural members of decks using pressure treated lumber or approved wood that is naturally resistant to decay. If pressure treated lumber is cut on-site, the cut ends should be treated with an approved wood preservative. Treated lumber, fir, cedar, and redwood may be used as deck top boards. Man-made composite material may be used as top boards also.

Recommendation: Perform an annual inspection of the deck and re-nail all loose boards and raised nails. Recoat the top boards with a good quality deck sealer every one or two years, depending upon the amount of exposure. Keep the underside of the deck free of debris and storage materials so that air can circulate underneath. The bottom of posts should be maintained 6 inches away from the soil. Landscape shrubs should not be allowed to grow around posts, as moisture may dry-rot posts.

DECK IS NOT FLASHED AT HOUSE/DECK CONNECTION

Decks attached to the house or other habitable structure should be flashed with an approved flashing material between the house and deck connection. Flashing should cover the top of the ledger completely and be sloped away from the house to prevent water from running between the back of the ledger and the exterior surface of the house. Building paper is not an acceptable flashing material.

Resolution: Install deck ledgers with an approved flashing material that runs behind the water resistant membrane, behind the exterior surface of the house, and over the top edge of the ledger.

NAIL HEADS OR SCREWS PROTRUDE ABOVE THE SURFACE OF THE DECK BOARDS

At the time of the walkthrough, nail heads, screws, or other fasteners that protrude above the deck board surface by more than 1/16-inch are considered non-performing.

Resolution: Re-nail or screw fasteners at the time of the walkthrough.

Recommendation: After the walkthrough, re-nailing or screw tightening of deck boards is a homeowner maintenance item. Deck boards shrink as they dry out, and they also move up and down with seasonal temperature changes. If the deck has wooden railings, the rail post bolts should be tightened every 6 months during the first two years of occupancy as a safety precaution.

PATIO SURFACES CRACK AND SEPARATE

Patios and decks should be constructed on soils and sub-surfaces that are properly drained and compacted sufficiently to prevent excessive movement. Deck and patios that should be constructed to slope away from the house with a slope of 1/4-inch per foot. Cracks in hard surfaces (such as concrete) exceeding 1/4-inch in width, or 1/4-inch in vertical displacement, are unacceptable. Modular pavers are subject to individual differential settlement, but should not have surfaces that are vertically offset by more than 1/4-inch from one paver to the adjoining one.

Resolution: Maintain all drainage courses and catch basins so that they are free of dirt, leaves and other debris. Do not apply heavy loads on deck surfaces.

FINISHED CONCRETE SURFACE HAS A BLOTCHY/MOTTLED COLOR

Assuming that each batch of concrete has been prepared with the same amount of color additive, non-uniform surface color on concrete is considered acceptable.

Resolution: None

Recommendation: Homeowner can speed up the process of equalizing the color by brushing the concrete with a wire broom, which will allow the air to react with the darker areas

WINDOWS AND PATIO DOORS

GLASS IS SCRATCHED OR BROKEN

At the time of delivery, glass that is visibly scratched or broken from a line of sight from 11 feet under daylight conditions (but not direct sunlight) is unacceptable. Damage to glass after the homeowner takes deliver of the house is not a Builder responsibility. Same applies to screens.

Resolution: Replace broken or scratched glass or screens if noted at the time of delivery of the house.

Recommendation: Homeowner should take care to inspect all windows and patio doors prior to delivery of the house, especially on house that have stucco as an exterior finish. Sand from the stucco may find its way onto the glass, and window washers can accidentally make small scratches in the glass when they are trying to clean it. Never use an abrasive cleaner on glass.

GLASS HAS IMPERFECTIONS

Imperfections that are part of the manufacturing process (as opposed to scratches), such as waviness and "cat's eye", which are visible from a distance of 6 feet under normal lighting conditions, are considered unacceptable.

Resolution: Builder should replace the glass.

WINDOWS AND PATIO DOORS ARE DIFFICULT TO OPEN AND CLOSE

All windows and patio doors should open and close freely ("freely" means without having to exert undue pressure or force by an adult of average strength). All latches and locks should operate in a similar manner.

Resolution: All window and door operating mechanisms, including latches and locks, should operate smoothly, without sticking or jamming, assuming that there is appropriate homeowner maintenance. Builder should adjust and/or otherwise correct malfunctioning mechanisms. Window and patio door operational problems caused by foundation of frame problems are also the responsibility of the Builder. Any damage that is caused by misuse or lack of proper maintenance by the homeowner should not be the responsibility of the Builder.

Recommendation: Windows and patio doors installed in houses today require little maintenance. Wood framed doors and windows have a tendency to "stick" during the winter months because the house takes on moisture, thereby expanding slightly; this is acceptable. Lubricating the rollers and slides with an approved window lubricant and adjusting the rollers on the patio doors are simple and routine maintenance items. Also, homeowners should brush and vacuum window and door tracks routinely.

WINDOW IS FOGGED BETWEEN PANES OF GLASS

Dual glazed window/door seals should not rupture during the manufacturer's warranty period, providing there is no misuse by the homeowner.

Resolution: Within the warranty period, Builder should assist the homeowner in dealing with the manufacturer to replace windows and patio doors whose seals have failed. This excludes failures caused by homeowner negligence or misuse.

Recommendation: Many homeowners unknowingly cause window seal failure by tinting the inside pane. This causes excessive heat buildup between the panes of glass and the seals are likely to rupture.

WINDOW GRIDS DISINTEGRATE

Window grids should not disintegrate or drop down inside the dual panes.

Resolution: Builder should replace window glass panel whose grids have failed. Exception: if homeowner has tinted the inside of the windows or otherwise caused the condition, Builder shall not be responsible for failed grids.

Recommendation: Do not tint the inside pane of dual pane windows.

WINDOW/PATIO DOOR LEAKS AT TOP OR BOTTOM

Windows should not leak at any point regardless of the location of the leak

Resolution: If the condition is a result of improper/inadequate construction, Builder should make repairs to eliminate the non-performing condition.

Recommendation: Homeowner should annually inspect and clean debris from all windows and patio door weep holes and caulk all inside corners of the sill. This maintenance is especially important in geographic areas that have trees with small leaves and also areas that experience dust storms. Patios and decks should be constructed 2 inches below the patio door threshold.

WINDOWS LEAK WHEN THE WIND BLOWS HARD

Use of residential windows and doors that are labeled with the appropriate AAMA "R"-rating for the geographical area is the guideline for rain and wind intrusion. For example, an oceanfront house should usually have windows and doors with a higher "R" rating than a house in a wooded valley.

Resolution: Builder should install windows and patio doors that meet the appropriate AAMA standards for the geographic area where the house is built. If this standard is met, the intrusion of wind-driven rain during extreme weather conditions is acceptable.

FRENCH DOORS AND OTHER EXTERIOR DOORS

WATER ENTERS WALLS AND INTERIOR THROUGH TOP, JAMBS AND THRESHOLD

Water entering through top, sides, bottom, or under door is considered unacceptable, unless the water is a result of excessive wind-driven rain. Pedestrian garage doors are not covered by this Guideline and are often installed without a sill.

Resolution: Builder repairs any exterior door that leaks as a result of improper original installation.

Recommendation: Keep threshold weeps and other drainage paths clean and free of obstructions and debris. If exterior door trim and joints between the doorframe and the exterior wall surface are caulked, inspect caulking annually and re-caulk (including the threshold) as necessary to maintain a weather-tight seal. Keep doors closed during wet weather. Depending upon geographic location and exposure, the weather-strips at the doors will need to be replaced between three and five years. Many doors have adjustable weather stripping at the bottom. When looking outside under the door bottom, daylight is visible, adjust the weather stripping by loosening the four or five screws on the bottom weather strip metal bar, and gently push the bar down so the strip under the door meets the threshold. Retighten the screws.

DOORS ARE WARPED, OUT-OF-LEVEL, NOT PLUMB

The vertical and horizontal planes of the door should not vary from a true plane by more than ¼ inch. Doors should not be installed out of true level and plumb by more than 1/8 inch. French door leaves should be installed in alignment with each other. Doors should remain in any position in which they are placed without closing or opening by themselves. If doors do move, it is an indication that they are out of plumb.

Resolution: Install doors within the Performance Guideline set forth above, and in adherence of the door manufacturer's installation requirements. Ensure that door components subject to moisture exposure are completely and effectively protected as soon as possible after the initial installation. The Builder is responsible for correcting any material, workmanship or inadequate design that results in improper door performance.

Recommendation: Do not place any load on door leaves, as they are not designed for this purpose and may sag over time. Keep door leaves and frames in good condition by repainting and re-caulking on a periodic basis. Adhere to the manufacturer's recommendation. Sometimes it is necessary to correct the fit of wood doors, either because of minor swelling or because surrounding finishes was replaced with materials of different thickness (for example, floor coverings). Any such corrections should be done professionally, and any bare wood should be immediately and completely sealed. If the bottom of a door is cut due to a change in flooring material, the fresh cut should be sealed.

CORROSION OR STAINING OF EXTERIOR HARDWARE

Hardware exposed to exterior atmospheric conditions should be corrosion-resistant. Hardware exposed to salt air in marine environment, or air containing corrosives from pollutants, should be made of materials suitable for use in such environments (for example, stainless steel).

Resolution: Install appropriate hardware for the specific environmental exposure of the House.

Recommendation: First, read the manufacturer's maintenance and care recommendations. Keep hardware clean and bright by polishing on a regular basis with a clean, soft cloth. Do not allow dust and other deleterious materials to accumulate. To preserve the factory-applied coating, avoid any abrasive products such as cleaners of polishing pads. While good care will extend the life of brass coatings, they will eventually break down and dark spots may appear. When tarnish reaches an undesirable level, the hardware should be removed from the door and the remaining lacquer coating completely removed. Coating removal should be done in accordance with the manufacturer's recommendations.

CHIMNEY AND FLUES

CHIMNEY CAP DOES NOT DRAIN

Chimney caps should be built so that tops have sufficient slope to avoid ponding of water.

Resolution: Builder should correct any improperly installed cap that is non-performing.

Recommendation: The Homeowner should include an inspection of the chimney cap and flue termination whenever the chimney flue is maintained by a professional cleaning service. Promptly notify the Builder of any problem identified. If the original installation secured the chimney cap through the horizontal surface of the chase cover, the Homeowner must periodically check the caulking of the attachment screw to avoid water penetration. The chimney cap is not designed to carry a person's weight, and standing upon the cap may cause it to collapse.

FLUE ENCLOSURE OPENS FOR ENTIRE HEIGHT (THROUGH FLOORS AND CEILINGS)

Flue enclosures should be blocked with sheet metal fitted to the opening and the flue where passing through floors and ceilings. These sheet metal assemblies are called draft stops.

Resolution: Builder should retrofit any draft stops missing from original construction.

Recommendation: Chimneys are supposed to be completely enclosed, and therefore cannot be inspected readily. If missing draft stops are discovered in the course of inspection or other work, the Homeowner should notify the builder.
IN THE CHIMNEY, WATER RUNS DOWN THE OUTSIDE OF THE FLUE

Where the flue exits through the chimney cap, a storm collar should be installed to deflect water away from penetration. Water should not run down the outside of the flue. During periods of high wind driven rain, some leakage is to be expected and is acceptable.

Resolution: If storm collar is missing or leaks, Builder should make the necessary corrections to meet the above Guideline.

Recommendation: Promptly bring any leak to the attention of the Builder, excepting leaks during periods of high wind driven rain.

FIREPLACE DOES NOT DRAW PROPERLY

Fireplace and chimney assemblies should be sized and installed in a manner that permits smoke and other products of combustion to exit freely through the flue, without putting any smoke into the room.

Resolution: If the condition is a result of improper installation, Builder should make any necessary corrections to achieve proper airflow in the flue. It is advisable to consult the fireplace manufacturer for their recommendations regarding flue diameter, permissible flue offsets, the shape and size of flue terminations, etc., as these factors may vary according to the type of system installed.

Recommendation: Dirty Flues can cause poorly drawing fireplaces. Also, overloading the fireplace with too much fuel may cause both smoke and dire to enter the room. Never burn newspapers of gift-wrappings, etc. If glass doors are installed as part of the House, they must be closed during burning operation. Fireplaces that do not have glass doors should not have them added unless specifically approved by the manufacturer.

GUTTERS AND DOWNSPOUTS

STANDING WATER IN GUTTERS AFTER RAINFALL

Gutters, if installed, should be installed with a downward slope (1/16-inch per three lineal feet) in the direction of the nearest downspout, if the frame of the House permits such installation. Alternatively, gutters may be installed level with downspouts. Gutters and/or downspouts should be installed in a manner that permits water to drain or evaporate completely from gutters within a period of no greater than 24 hours after the cessation of rainfall in summer and 36 hours in winter. This time period shall be extended if weather conditions such as heavy winter fog or snow persist in the region. No part of any gutter should be installed with a back-slope (sloping away from the nearest downspout).

Resolution: Builder should correct either the slope of the gutter or add more downspouts.

Recommendation: Homeowner should keep gutters free of leaves, toys, or other debris. The slope of a level gutter can easily be unfavorably reversed by allowing debris to accumulate. Acid produced by decaying leaves will, over time, eat through a metal gutter. Gutters should be cleaned annually and more frequently if mature trees are adjacent to the House.

GUTTER JOINTS LEAK / DOWNSPOUT JOINTS LEAK

Gutter and downspout joints should be assembled so that they do not leak.

Resolution: Builder should make repairs to seams in gutters and downspouts that leak.

Recommendation: None

GUTTER ENDS ARE EMBEDDED IN WALL SURFACE MATERIAL

Gutters should not be embedded into stucco and should terminate no closer than one-inch from the surface of intersecting walls.

Resolution: If gutter ends are embedded or are too tight to wall surface materials, they should be rebuilt or corrected by the builder.

Recommendation: None.

GUTTERS OVERFLOW

The Builder should size gutters so that they do not overflow under normal rainfall conditions. The frequency and cross sectional area of down spouts should be adequate to serve the computed maximum flow of storm water as defined by the SMACNA architectural sheet metal manual. The shapes of gutters should be selected so that water flowing off the roof is intercepted by the gutter and does not wash over the front edge of the gutter. Water falling from upper roofs directly onto lower roofs without gutters is acceptable.

Resolution: If overflow is a result of improper or inadequate installation and not from inadequate Homeowner maintenance, builder should make necessary adjustments so that gutters do not overflow during periods of heavy rainfall.

Recommendation: Annual maintenance of gutters and downspouts is important to avoid leaks and prolong the life of the system. Gutters should be cleaned thoroughly. If the House is in an area with mature trees, it is a good idea to place gutter screens along the gutter length and in the top opening of each downspout to help minimize leaf debris. If a gutter or downspout leaks, have it repaired at the first opportunity. If gutters are made of galvanized sheet metal their useful life will be greatly reduced if the Homeowner allows acidic bird droppings, eucalyptus leaves or pine needles to accumulate in the gutter.

GUTTERS DO NOT EXTEND FULLY TO THE GABLE ENDS OF THE ROOF

Gutters should provide complete coverage along the roof eave. However, the Builder may elect to install gutters only on a portion of the House, such as over an exterior doorway or patio. The Builder is not required by Code to install gutters, unless it is required by local ordinance.

Resolution: Unless the architectural design of the House shows otherwise, gutters should run completely along the eave. An exception to this is the use of a Dutch gutter, or diverter, at certain locations to divert rainwater to other areas (i.e. over an entryway).

Recommendation: Do not alter the finished grades around the House that were provided by the Builder unless done according to Code and as directed by a licensed landscape architect or civil engineer. Keep all drainage swales free of debris. If the House has one, flush out the underground pipe system with a garden hose prior to the start of the rainy season.

DOWNSPOUT MAKES "PINGING" NOISE DURING RAIN STORMS

Due to many factors beyond the control of Builder, such as architectural design, rainwater collection requirements, and varying degrees of annoyance threshold by the occupants, the Builder is not responsible for downspout noise.

Resolution: None

Recommendation: If downspout noise exists to the extent and/or in a location that affects the quality of habitability (such as outside bedroom window) the following suggestions can mitigate the noise:

-If the bottom of downspout is "kicked out" from the wall and is not inserted into a collection pipe, glue a piece of carpet padding into the kicked out portion. Make sure the metal is clean and dry and use watertight glue. Inspect the discharge during the rainy season to keep it cleared of any leaves of debris.

-If the downspout has several twists and turns and the bottom is not accessible, hang a galvanized steel or plastic chain with one-inch wide links into the top 3 to 5 feet of the downspout. Hang the top link from a copper or brass rod that is at least 12 inches long. It is important that the chain and the rod be made of material that does not rust. Inspect the chain frequently during the rainy season and clean it as necessary.

SKYLIGHTS

SKYLIGHT LEAKS

Skylights should be installed so they do not leak. Skylights may leak as a result of failures in the frame or glazing, or more commonly because of incorrect installation.

Resolution: Improperly installed skylights should be reset and properly waterproofed. The Builder should be responsible for administering any manufacturer's warranty work in the event of a failure of the skylight assembly.

Recommendation: None.

MOISUTRE CONDENSES ON INTERIOR SURFACES OF THE SKYLIGHT

Moisture condensation on the interior surface of skylight glazing is considered acceptable. However, condensation moisture that is excessive and finds its way into surrounding finishes and cavities is unacceptable. Skylight perimeters must be detailed so that condensation water is adequately trapped in an impervious gutter or similar detail, where it can rest until it has a chance to evaporate.

Resolution: Improperly detailed skylight perimeters should be reconstructed so that condensation water is adequately trapped and allowed to evaporate.

Recommendation: Homeowner assumes responsibility for the amount of humidity created in kitchens, baths, laundry rooms and other areas or devices that produce water vapor.

MOISTURE APPEARS BETWEEN THE PANES OF A DUAL PANE SKYLIGHT

Moisture trapped between the panes of a dual pane skylight indicates a broken seal. This is unacceptable.

Resolution: If the broken seal occurs within the manufacturer's warranty period, Builder should replace the skylight glazing.

Recommendation: Do not tint the inside surface of a skylight, as the warranty may be voided.

SKYLIGHT ADMITS TOO MUCH HEAT

A House with skylights must conform to energy conservation standards. Assuming energy calculations have been done correctly, heat gain through a skylight is considered acceptable.

Resolution: Builder installed skylights should conform to appropriate energy requirements, and the energy calculations for the House.

Recommendation: Homeowner can install heat reflecting or absorbing systems according to their own taste and in accordance with the manufacturer's recommendations.

PAINT AND STAIN

STAINS FROM UNDERLYING SURFACES BLEED THROUGH

Colors, markings, wood sap, tannins, etc. which are on the surface of or are within the composition of underlying materials should not bleed through to the surface of the paint.

Resolution: Builder should ensure that surfaces to which paints and stains are applied are properly prepared and cleaned. If components of an underlying material have an inherent tendency to bleed through, The Builder should apply stain blocking coatings or primers before proceeding with painting or staining.

Recommendation: None.

PAINT BECOMES CHALKS OR FADES

Paint should not chalk or fade within the period of time that the manufacturer warrants its performance from such deterioration.

Resolution: Builder should select paints and stains that are suitable for the exposure and climate zone for the House.

Recommendation: It is important to observe the condition of painted surfaces on a periodic basis. An annual inspection is recommended. Paints first begin to show signs of wear in limited areas. Maintenance and touch up should be undertaken before paint degradation proceeds too far. This can significantly extend the life of the overall paint job.

PAINT FLAKING OR PEELING

Paint should not flake or peel during the manufacturer's warranted life of the product.

Resolution: Builder should ensure that appropriate paint selections are made, and that surfaces are properly prepared to receive paints. In the case of premature flaking or peeling, the Builder should take appropriate action to remediate the non-performing condition, up to and including stripping and repainting affected surfaces, as may be required to provide a durable finish.

Recommendation: Maintain paint surfaces in a clean and well-ventilated condition. Inspect painted surfaces periodically and touch up any initial onset of premature aging or deterioration that may be observed.

PAINTS APPLED TOO THIN, TOO TICK, OR IN A SPOTTY MANNER

All surfaces to receive pain should uniformly coated without any unpainted or too lightly painted spots called "holidays" in the painting trade. Paint coatings should be applied to at least the minimum thickness recommended by the manufacturer. Paint should not be applied too thick, which usually results in spots that are more reflective than surrounding surfaces called "shiners." Paint should be applied smoothly and evenly, without any runs or drips.

Resolution: The Builder should conform to the Performance Guideline. Any areas that are not painted in conformance to the Guideline should be repainted properly.

Recommendation: None.

PAINT OR STAIN OVERSPRAY ON ADJACENT SURFACES

Over spray of paints or stains on surfaces that are not intended to receive paint or stain coatings is not acceptable. Over spray must be clearly visible at a distance of five feet under normal natural lighting conditions to be non-performing.

Resolution: Builder should take measures to protect surfaces that are not to be painted and which may be subject to overspray damage. If overspray occurs despite protective measures, Builder should clean the affected areas in a manner that does not damage the affected surfaces.

Recommendation: None.

MILDEW OR FUNGI GROWTH / STAINS ON PAINTED SURFACES

Mildew and fungi that affect exterior surfaces may be difficult or impossible to avoid in some particularly moist and cool locations and therefore are not considered a condition of non-performance. Molds and mildews that appear on interior surfaces, and are the result of leaks, are considered unacceptable. Interior surfaces similarly affected by condensation may either be considered unacceptable or a Homeowner maintenance item, depending upon circumstances.

Resolution: Builder is responsible for selection of paints that are reasonably resistant to the establishment and spread of mildews and fungi on exterior walls. Paints are now formulated with mildewcide and fungicide additives that inhibit the growth of mildew and fungi. The Builder should use these types of products on exterior walls when the orientation and climate at the home site indicates their use is necessary. At interior walls, if mildews and molds become established as a consequence of leaks in the exterior walls, roof above, or any other building component, it should be the Builder's responsibility to correct the leaks, and to clean up and restore any affected areas (if leaks are a result of improper construction).

Recommendation: Homeowner should periodically inspect exterior surfaces to determine if mildew or fungus growth is occurring. Any growth of these organisms should be addressed by the proper cleaning and application of products that will kill the organisms and retard their return. This should be done promptly upon observation of mildews or fungi, because once established, these organisms are progressively more difficult to control and eradicate. At interior locations, the Homeowner should always use the mechanical ventilation in bathrooms, laundry rooms, and kitchens while these rooms are in use, and regularly air out rooms that have windows. If the Homeowner observes significant condensation on exterior surfaces (usually at windows and cool exterior walls), an effort should be made to find the right balance of natural and mechanical ventilation to minimize the problem.

LACQUERS AND VARNISHES PEEL AND FLAKE RAPIDLY

Clear exterior lacquer and varnish coatings are not recommended for use on exterior surfaces. They usually deteriorate rapidly and require substantial maintenance. Deteriorated exterior varnishes and lacquers are not considered acceptable. Interior varnished and lacquered surfaces may be appropriate, provided that they are not applied in locations subject to extensive direct sunlight or excessive moisture.

Resolution: Interior lacquers and varnishes that peel or flake off, and are not subject to Homeowner abuse or excessive moisture, should be corrected by the Builder.

Recommendation: Homeowner should keep all varnished and lacquered surfaces reasonably free of excessive moisture, heat, dust, and from other damaging conditions. Relatively frequent maintenance and recoating with a high quality marine spray varnish should be anticipated and performed by the Homeowner.

STAINED EXTERIOR SURFACES ARE BLOTCHY OR HAVE UNEVEN COLOR

Stains are absorbed by wood to different degrees, depending on the prevalence of sapwood, knots, and the character of the tree from which the wood product was made, Stains on synthetic surfaces may be more regular, but some variation is still inevitable. Stained surfaces, however, should not be excessively blotchy, or vary markedly in color.

Resolution: Builder should prepare surfaces and apply stains in strict accordance with the manufacturer's directions and recommendations, and in a manner that minimizes extreme variations in color or blotchiness. Surfaces that are not in conformance should be cleaned and re-coated in a manner that achieves a reasonable degree of regularity.

Recommendation: Homeowner is responsible for maintaining the stained surfaces clean and free of debris. Adequate ventilation of exposed surfaces should be provided. Homeowner should recoat stained surfaces at an interval no longer than what is recommended by the manufacturer.

PAINTED STUCCO SURFACES DO NOT PERMIT MOISTURE TO ESCAPE

Stucco surfaces that are designed to receive paint should be painted with materials that allow water vapor to pass from the inner surface to the outer surface. The use of impermeable membrane paints in considered unacceptable for this application.

Resolution: Apply only breathable surface coatings to stucco exteriors. Apply according to the methods and thickness recommended by the manufacturer.

Recommendation: None.
BRUSH MARKS OR LAP MARKS SHOW

When viewed in normal daylight at a distance of 6 feet, brush marks or lap marks should not be visible. Artificial light is not acceptable as a light source when measuring this Guideline.

Resolution: Builder should make corrections to non-conforming items.

Recommendation: None.

BRICK AND MASONRY

CHIMNEY IS CRACKED

Cracks in mortar joints in excess of 1/8-inch are not acceptable. Cracks that run through the brick or stone (as opposed to mortar joints) in excess of 1/8-inch are not acceptable. Cracks that run through both the mortar joints and the brick or stone in excess of 3/8-inch are not acceptable; they may be the telltale sign of an underlying structural deficiency.

Resolution: Builder shall make repairs by tuck-pointing the masonry cracks. Bricks or stone that are cracked in excess of 1/8-inch shall be replaced. Any cracks that are greater than 3/8-inch shall be investigated by a structural professional and the Builder shall perform his or her recommended repair.

Recommendation: None.

MASONRY WALL OR MASONRY VENNER IS CRACKED

Cracks in excess of 1/8-inch are considered non-performing.

Resolution: For all non-performing conditions, Builder shall tuck-point cracks in mortar joints, and replace brick or stone or CMU's if they are cracked in excess of 1/8-inch.

Recommendation: Homeowner shall not alter the finish grade around any masonry wall. All rainwater should flow away from the wall.
CUT BRICKS BELOW OPENINGS IN MASONRY WALLS ARE DIFFERENT THICKNESS

Cut bricks used in the course directly below an opening in a masonry wall shall be uniform in size to a tolerance of 1/4-inch. In addition there shall be no brick pieces or "chips" that are smaller than one inch in any direction.

Resolution: Builder shall remove and replace any condition that is not performing.

Recommendation: None.

BRICK OR CMU COURSES ARE NOT STRAIGHT AND MORTAR JOINTS VARY IN THICKNESS

Using a line of sight along a mortar joint, the mortar joint must be within 1/2-inch of the same elevation from beginning to end. Additionally, the mortar joint may not vary in thickness by more than 1/4-inch in 10 feet of length.

Resolution: Builder shall correct non-performing walls.

Recommendation: None.

BRICK IS DISINTEGRATING (SPALLING)

New brick that spalls or disintegrates is unacceptable. This guideline includes manufactured used brick. Actual used brick may exhibit some superficial spalling, and as long as at least 90% of the volume of the brick remains intact, it is considered acceptable.

Resolution: Replace brick that does not conform.

Recommendation: Brush and wash off the white powdery substance (efflorescence) that sometimes appears on brick surfaces during wet weather.

INTERIOR COMPONENTS

FIREPLACES

WATER DRIPS INTO FIREPLACE DURING RAINSTORMS

Water should not drip into the fireplace during normal rainstorms. However, rainwater may pass down the chimney into the fireplace during extreme wind driven storms.

Resolution: If water drips into the fireplace during normal or light rainstorms, it is most likely due to a seam leak at the chase cover or the rain cap. The Builder should repair the leak.

Recommendation: Keep the damper closed when the fireplace is not in use. Note: if the fireplace is used for burning wood, be certain there are no live coals or embers before closing the damper. Otherwise, poisonous gases could enter the room. The flue must be cleaned (swept) periodically from the top, going downward, in accordance with the manufacturer's instructions and according to the amount of use of the fireplace. Failure to keep the chimney clean can result in dangerous flue fires high up in the chimney. Special chimney cleaning logs are now available, and their manufacturer claims they accomplish the same task as a chimney sweep.

FIREPLACE WON'T DRAW (ROOM BECOMES SMOKY)

Fireplaces should be constructed so that ass gases from combustion are carried out the chimney or flue.

Resolution: Fireplace assembly including firebox, flue, external combustion air vents, chimney, and termination cap should be constructed in accordance with the Code and the fireplace manufacturer's installation instructions.

Recommendation: Always be sure the damper is open before starting a fire. Do not overload the firebox with too much fuel or improper fuel (such as paper, trash, etc.). Use only the fuel that is approved by the manufacturer (a gas log fireplace is typically not suited to burn wood or paper). If installed, glass doors should be closed during fireplace operation.

REFRACTORY PANELS CRACK

Refractory panels that crack more than 1/16-inch or crack to the extent that the panel breaks into pieces during the warranty period are considered unacceptable.

Resolution: Builder should replace cracked refractory panels if damage is not a result of improper use by Homeowner.

Recommendation: Homeowner should "cure" new refractory panels by building a series of small, low-heat fires before fully using the entire fireplace. It is important to read the owner's instruction manual and avoid creating high heat fires with items such as paper, composition logs, or lumber. Always place logs into the firebox using metal tongs; logs thrown into the firebox may hit the refractory panels and cause it to crack. Avoid burning any composite wood material such as particleboard or glulam beam scraps.

DAMPER BECOMES DUSTY

The damper should be free of rust and operate smoothly at the time of the Walkthrough.

Resolution: Meet the Guideline.

Recommendation: Dampers will become rusty because water is formed when any type of fuel is burned. It is normal to expect some rust on the damper and its hinges. If the damper becomes difficult to operate, the hinges can be sprayed with a rust removing lubricant. Do not spray when there is a fire or hot coals present. The spray may be flammable.

GLASS DOORS DO NOT OPERATE FREELY

At the time of delivery, glass fireplace doors should open and close freely without sticking, and should close with a gap of no more than 1/4-inch when closed.

Resolution: Builder should make necessary repairs or adjustments so that the glass doors operate in conformance with the above Guideline.

Recommendation: None. However, glass doors should remain closed during fireplace operation.

INSULATION

THERE IS NO INSULATION IN THE ATTIC

Some insulation should be present in every attic that is built over habitable space, unless another package approved by the building department exists instead. Occasionally, on desert style homes with "flat" roofs and no attic, part of the roof assembly is made of insulating foam, and this qualifies as ceiling/roof insulation.

Resolution: All insulation should be the R-Values as specified in the Title 24 compliance section of the building permit.

Recommendation: None.

INSULATION IS PLACED AGAINST THE EAVE VENTS OR THE FOUNDATION VENTS

Insulation should not be placed against the eave (attic) or foundation vents. Clear space (between one to two feet) should be left between the end of the insulation and the vent screen to allow for proper air circulation.

Resolution: The Builder should remove any originally installed insulation that blocks the airflow of eave and foundation vents.

Recommendation: None.

HOUSE IS TOO HOT IN SUMMER, TOO COLD IN WINTER

Each new House must be built in compliance with local Energy Codes. There is no guarantee that an individual level of comfort will be met.

Resolution: None, provided the House has been built in compliance with the appropriate section of the applicable Energy Code.

Recommendation: Much of the comfort a House provides depends on the lifestyle of the occupants. For example, it is unrealistic to expect that an air conditioner turned on a 5pm on a hot summer day could effectively and entirely cool the House by bedtime. Additionally, in wintertime furnaces should be programmed to come on in the morning at least 30 minutes before the time the occupants wake. Constant adjustments to the thermostat will result in uneven temperatures and periods of discomfort. Also, installation of insulating drapes and shades is an important way to increase House comfort and decrease energy consumption.

INSULATION BATTS DO NOT FIT TIGHT TO THE FRAMING MEMBERS

In order to achieve maximum insulation performance, the batts must be installed tight to the framing members without gaps. This also includes tight fits around plumbing lines and electrical boxes.

Resolution: If loose fitting insulation is present, Builder shall make appropriate adjustments to close any gaps in insulation.

Recommendation: None.

INTERIOR DOORS

DOOR IS WARPED

Doors that are warped more than 1/4-inch in a 6 foot 8-inch height are considered unacceptable.

Resolution: Builder should replace doors that are warped in excess of the above Performance Guideline.

Recommendation: None.
DOOR PANELS HAVE SPLIT

Door panels that have split entirely through and allow light to pass through are considered unacceptable.

Resolution: Make necessary repairs to meet the above Performance Guideline.

Recommendation: None.

DOOR HANGS CROOKED IN JAMB

Doors that vary more than 1/4-inch in measurement from the closest distance to the jamb to the furthest distance to the jamb or head are considered unacceptable.

Resolution: Builder should make the necessary adjustments to the door or jamb to meet the Performance Guideline, if condition is a result of improper or inadequate installation.

Recommendation: Do not hang anything heavy on doors or doorknobs. This can pull the top hinges out of adjustment and negatively affect the door swing.

DOOR LATCH DOES NOT ENGAGE IN THE STRIKE PLATE

Door latches should engage firmly in the strike plate.

Resolution: Builder should make the necessary adjustments to meet the Guideline, if condition is a result of improper or inadequate installation.

Recommendation: Do not hang anything heavy on doors or doorknobs. This can pull the top hinges out of adjustment and negatively affect the door swing.

DOOR OPENS OR CLOSES BY ITSELF

Doors should stay open when opened, and stay closed when closed. "Phantom" openings and closings are considered unacceptable.

Resolution: Builder should make the necessary adjustments to meet the Guideline, if condition is a result of improper or inadequate installation.

Recommendation: Do not hang anything heavy on doors or doorknobs. This can pull the top hinges out of adjustment and negatively affect the door swing. Seasonal humidity changes can result in impaired door swing performance; this is acceptable.

BOTTOM EDGE OF DOOR IS CUT TOO HIGH OR TOO LOW

A door that swings over carpeted areas should not drag on the carpet. Doors should be cut to leave a gap of no longer than 1 inch above the uppermost tufts of the carpet. A door that swings over a non-carpeted surface should be cut to leave a gap of no larger than 1/2-inch above the floor surface. Exception: Doors opening to utility areas, such as laundry rooms and pantries may have a gap up to 1-3/8-inches from the finish floor. This condition arises when vinyl flooring is glued to a concrete slab, and it is considered acceptable.

Resolution: Builder should make the necessary adjustments to meet the Guideline, if condition is a result of improper or inadequate installation.

Recommendation: If the Homeowner changes the type or texture of finish flooring or provides his or her own finish flooring, the Builder is not responsible for making door adjustments.

POCKET DOOR BINDS BETWEEN THE POCKETS

Door should not rub and/or bind in their pockets during normal operation.

Resolution: The Builder should furnish and install all pocket doors to meet the above Guideline. If the door does not operate as such, the Builder should repair as necessary and refinish any work damaged by the subject repairs.

Recommendation: Operate the doors in a normal fashion and do not negligently slam the doors back and forth.

DOOR HARDWARE

DOORKNOB MECHANISM OPERATES STIFFLY

Door latch mechanisms should operate smoothly without requiring a great deal of effort to disengage the strike plate or deadbolt.

Resolution: Builder should repair or replace any unacceptable door latch mechanisms whose improper performance is not a result of lack of Homeowner maintenance or misuse.

Recommendation: Door latch mechanisms should be lubricated annually with a dry lubricant made for door latch mechanisms.

DOORKNOB FINISH TARNISHES

Doorknobs may tarnish over time. This is a Homeowner maintenance item.

Resolution: Builder should replace only those doorknobs that are tarnished at the time of the Walkthrough.

Recommendation: Learn about the proper care of metal finishes, especially bright brass, and conduct appropriate maintenance for the particular metal finish. If the House is located in a marine environment, expect pitting and tarnishing of the hardware finishes unless the hardware is labeled "lifetime finished". In all cases, refer to the manufacturer's warranty and maintenance requirements.

CLOSETS

POLES PULL OUT OF ROSETTES

Closet poles should fit firmly into rosettes, and should not be held away from the inside end of the rosette by more than 1/8-inch. Poles should have an intermediate support for every four feet of length.

Resolution: Builder should make necessary repairs to meet the above Guideline.

Recommendation: Do not overload closet poles with heavy clothing or too much clothing. This will cause the pole to deflect and pull out of the rosette.

FINISH FLOORING

FLOOR NOT LEVEL, FLOOR SQUEAKS, EXCESSIVE DEFLECTION (SAGGING), EXCESSIVE FELEXIBILITY (BOUNCE)

Finish floors should not deviate more than 1/4-inch from true level in a horizontal distance of 8 feet. No point in the surface of a floor should be more than 1/8-inch above or below the plane of the floor. Squeaks are usually the result of separate parts of the floor moving relative to each other and rubbing against nails. Floors should be designed to accommodate Building Code required live loads.

Resolution: Builder should repair or replace finish flooring that deviates from the above guideline, if condition is a result of improper or inadequate installation and not a result of Homeowner misuse.

Recommendation: Maintain flooring using products and methods approved by the manufacturer and/ or trade association whose products have been installed. Avoid overloading floors. Consult with the Builder or a qualified engineer prior to placing exceptionally heavy objects on a floor to ensure the floor load capacity will not be exceeded. If the Homeowner installs a finish floor, the Homeowner assumes complete responsibility for the conation of the subfloor or slab at the time of installation and thereafter.

HARDWOOD FLOORING

CUPPING OR CROWNING OF INDIVIDUAL FLOOR BOARDS

Hardwood flooring should be installed in a manner that will prevent cupping and crowning. This includes, among other measures, proper acclimatization of floor material prior to installation and the use of suitable moisture barriers under the flooring. Cupping or crowning should not exceed 1/16-inch in a 3-inch span as measured across the individual board.

Resolution: If cupping or crowning exceeds the Guideline, the Builder should replace or repair the floor as necessary to meet the Guideline.

Recommendation: Always maintain hardwood floor in accordance with the manufacturer's recommendations, do not allow any spills or liquids to remain on floors, and do not clean floors with detergents. Use only those cleaning products recommended by the manufacturer. Some minor random cupping or crowning can be expected over the years due to changes in humidity, and this condition is acceptable.

SCALLEOPED AND ABRADED SURFACE

Wood floors should be finished without gouges, abrasions or scalloping. Some unevenness can be expected because portions of the grain of wood are softer than others.

Resolution: Builder should repair or replace any non-performing boards noticed at the Walkthrough.

Recommendation: Any surface gouges and abrasions should be brought to the attention of the Builder at the Walkthrough and prior to the move-in. The Builder is not responsible for gouges and abrasions noticed after the Walkthrough. Always maintain hardwood floor in accordance with the manufacturer's recommendations, do not allow any spills or liquids to remain on floors, and do not clean floors with detergents. Use only those cleaning products recommended by the manufacturer.

GAPS BETWEEN ADJACENT FLOOR BOARDS

Manufactured (pre-finished) floors should be installed strictly in accordance with the manufacturer's instructions and should perform in accordance with the manufacturer's warranty. Floors finished in the field: floor joints should be tight and without gaps. Gaps between boards are the result of shrinkage. Although wood flooring materials are dried by the manufacturer, they still contain moisture. New wood floors should not be subjected to extreme variations in temperature or humidity. Gaps should not occur in more than 5% of the total length of joints in a floor, and no gap should exceed 1/32-inch in width for boards in excess of 2-1/4-inches in width.

Resolution: If gaps between boards exceed the Guideline, the Builder should replace or repair the floor as necessary to meet the Guideline.

Recommendation: Always maintain hardwood floor in accordance with the manufacturer's recommendations, do not allow any spills or liquids to remain on floors, and do not clean floors with detergents. Use only those cleaning products recommended by the manufacturer.

DIFFERENCES IN COLOR BETWEEN INDIVIDUAL FLOOR BOARDS

Wood floors naturally have color variation. The same species of wood may come in many different colors, floor boards may vary accordingly.

Resolution: None.

Recommendation: If uniformity of color is important, Homeowner should make advance arrangement with the Builder at the time the flooring section is completed, so that the Homeowner is present when the floor is being installed. Homeowner should be aware that direct sunlight can cause wood floors to become lighter; the Builder is not responsible for this condition. The floor areas under area rugs and large pieces of furniture will remain as the original wood or stain color (usually darker). Removal of the rug or relocation of the furniture will allow the floor to reach a uniform color.

FLOOR BOARDS ON PRE-FINISHED FLOORS ARE NOT LEVEL WITH ONE ANOTHER AT SIDES OR ENDS

Finish floorboards should not be higher or lower than the immediately adjoining board by more than .012-inch measured with a feeler gauge.

Resolution: Builder should make necessary repairs to meet the above guideline, unless condition is a result of a Homeowner misuse or improper maintenance.

Recommendation: Floor care is important. If water based liquid is spilled on the floor, or if areas of high humidity exist in poorly vented rooms, the floorboards may swell and become uneven. Builder is not responsible for this condition.

SPLINTERS OR CHIPS ARE PRESENT AT THE EDGES OF FLOOR BOARDS AFTER INSTALLATION

Whether the floor is pre-finished or sanded and finished in place, there should be no splinters or chips that could be caught in flesh or clothing after installation is complete.

Resolution: Repair or replace boards that do not meet the above guideline.

Recommendation: Floor care is important. Always maintain hardwood floor in accordance with the manufacturer's recommendations, do not allow any spills or liquids to remain on floors, and do not clean floors with detergents. Use only those cleaning products recommended by the manufacturer.

DARK LINES APPEAR PERPENDICULAR TO THE FLOOR BOARD

Sticker lines across floorboards that cannot be removed during the sanding process are considered unacceptable. To be considered unacceptable, the dark line should be clearly visible to the untrained eye at a distance of 6 feet under normal daylight conditions

Resolution: Replace or replace floorboards that do not meet the above Performance Guideline.

Recommendation: Always maintain hardwood floor in accordance with the manufacturer's recommendations, do not allow any spills or liquids to remain on floors, and do not clean floors with detergents. Use only those cleaning products recommended by the manufacturer.

FLOOR BOARDS DISCOLOR AND ROT, PARTICULARLY UNDER AREA RUGS

Floorboards should not discolor (turn very dark) and rot, or become brittle and crumble.

Resolution: Builder should make repairs unless the damage is caused by Homeowner misuse or negligence.

Recommendation: If the Homeowner covers a pre-finished hardwood floor with an area rug, he or she takes on the responsibility to monitor the condition of the wood on a quarterly basis (every three months). To avoid this, the area rug can be installed on the concrete slab with the wood floor around it. Homeowner should also be aware that direct sunlight will cause wood floors to become darker; the Builder is not responsible for this condition.

CERAMIC AND CLAY TILE FLOORING

CRACKS AND / OR LOOSE TILES

Tiles having cracks that are visible at a distance of 4 feet, and any loose tiles that can be moved by hand, are not acceptable.

Resolution: Builder should replace cracked tiles and reset loose tiles that do not meet the above guideline.

Recommendation: Homeowner should be aware that ceramic and clay tiles are brittle and they can be cracked, chipped or broken by placing or dropping heavy objects on them; the Builder is not responsible for the resulting conditions.

GROUT IS CRACKED

Hairline cracks can occur in grout and are considered acceptable. Cracks larger than 1/32 inch should be re-grouted as part of the Builder's Responsibility. If continual cracking occurs, the underlying floor may be deflecting. If this condition exists, it should be repaired.

Resolution: Builder should meet the Performance guideline by repairing or replacing any non-performing condition.

Recommendation: Homeowners should familiarize themselves with proper procedures for cleaning and caring for their tile floors. Grout is very porous and should be sealed by the Homeowner within 30 days of occupancy.

INDIVIDUAL TILES ARE OUT OF PLANE

This Guideline will vary depending upon the type of tile that is installed. Tiles can vary from flat ceramic, to rose, to uneven terra cotta. For tile that is flat, adjoining tiles should be no more than 1/16-inch higher or lower than the surrounding tiles. For tile that is handmade with uneven surfaces, the butts at the grout joints should not exceed 1/4-inch in elevation from surrounding tiles.

Resolution: Builder should repair or replace any non-performing tiles.

Recommendation: Homeowners should familiarize themselves with proper procedures for cleaning and caring for their tile floors.

GRANITE, MARBLE, AND OTHER STONE FLOORING

CRACKS

Granite, marble, and other stone are susceptible to hairline cracking. This is normal condition. Cracks in excess of 3/64-inch are unacceptable.

Resolution: Builder should repair or replace any non-conforming condition that is a result of initial construction, and is not a product of Homeowner misuse.

Recommendation: Examine floors carefully at time of the Walkthrough. Homeowner should not place unusually heavy items onto stone flooring, unless Builder was notified and has provided appropriate support.

STAINS

Builder should deliver a marble, granite, or other stone floor free of stains, with a consistent surface sheen or texture. The Homeowner should carefully examine the surface of the marble, granite, or other stone floor prior to taking possession of the House. The Builder will not accept responsibility for stained conditions if they are not noted at the time of the Walkthrough. Many times what may appear to be discolorations are actually natural variations in the stone.

Resolution: Builder should repair or replace the non-conforming condition if noted at the time of the Walkthrough.

Recommendation: None. Ensure that you careful examination of the floor during the Walkthrough.

SCRATCHES AND ABRASIONS

Homeowner should note any scratches and abrasions during the Walkthrough. The Builder should deliver a marble, granite, or other stone floor free of scratches and abrasions, with a consistent surface sheen or texture.

Resolution: Marble, granite, and tumbled stone will naturally have numerous pits and voids. Small pits are considered part of the "achieved look" of the surface and should not be deemed as non-preforming. The manufacturer or installer usually fills voids in excess of 3/8-inch in diameter.

Recommendation: None; careful examination of the floor during the Walkthrough.

VINYL FLOORING

WIDE SEAMS OR JOINTS

Sheet and tile resilient floors should be laid with tight joints. Any separation in excess of 1/32-inch is non-performing.

Resolution: Builder should make necessary repairs or replacements.

Recommendation: Homeowners should follow the flooring manufacturer's cleaning and care instructions for vinyl flooring.

DELAMINATION

Occasionally resilient floors will separate from the underlayment, particularly at edges. Such delamination is unacceptable and should be corrected by re-gluing.

Resolution: Builder should make necessary repairs or replacements.

Recommendation: Homeowners should follow the flooring manufacturer's cleaning and care instructions for vinyl flooring. To extend the life of vinyl flooring, use area rugs or mats at workstations and use dirt-trapping mats at exterior doors. Do not allow water or other liquids to remain on vinyl flooring for long periods of time. Spills or splashes should be promptly and properly removed. Vinyl flooring is water resistant and not totally waterproof.

DISCOLORATION

Floors should not become discolored as a result of moisture underneath the finish floor. If discoloration is a result of chemical and natural products with staining properties being allowed to remain on the surface of the resilient material without prompt cleaning, Builder is not responsible.

Resolution: Builder should make necessary repairs or replacements if condition is a result of moisture underneath the finish floor and not a result of Homeowner misuse or negligence.

Recommendation: Do not allow chemical or natural products with staining properties to remain on the finish floor. Homeowners should follow the flooring manufacturer's cleaning and care instructions for vinyl flooring. Do not allow water or other liquids to remain on vinyl flooring for long periods of time. Spills or splashes should be promptly and properly.

ADHESIVE APPEARS ON THE SURFACE THROUGH JOINTS

Adhesives should not appear through the surface around joints or seams.

Resolution: Builder should making necessary repairs or replacements. If after thorough cleaning with a manufacturer-approved cleaning agent the non-performing condition recurs, the floor should be removed along with the existing adhesive, and the floor re-laid by the Builder.

Recommendation: Homeowners should follow the flooring manufacturer's cleaning and care instructions for vinyl flooring.

"TELEGRAPHING" OR IRREGULAR SURFACE BEANEATH VINYL FLOORING

Various types of irregularities, such as cracks in concrete subfloors, or unevenness in subfloors, or trapped debris, may show through the resilient flooring observed at a distance of 6 ft. under normal lighting conditions, appearing as unsightly bumps and lines. These conditions are non-performing.

Resolution: Builder should making necessary repairs or replacements to non-performing conditions.

Recommendation: Homeowners should following the flooring manufacturer's cleaning and care instructions for vinyl flooring.

PATTERN DOES NOT MATCH OR ALIGN

Patterns should match or align within 1/8-inch in a six-foot length of flooring.

Resolution: Builder should make necessary repairs or replacements, assuming no damage or misuse by Homeowner.

Recommendation: Homeowners should follow the flooring manufacturer's cleaning and care instructions for vinyl flooring.

CARPET FLOORING

VISIBLE SEEMS

Visibility of carpet seams is acceptable unless the seam is not butted tightly, and the seaming tape shows.

Resolution: Builder should make the necessary repairs to meet the above Performance Guideline.

Recommendation: None. However, Homeowners should follow the flooring manufacturer's cleaning and care instructions.

CARPET IS LOOSE

Carpets should be stretched tightly, without areas of looseness. If the carpet is loose, the Builder should have it re-stretched.

Resolution: Builder should make the necessary repairs.

Recommendation: None. However, Homeowners should follow the flooring manufacturer's cleaning and care instructions.

CARPET FIBERS SEPARATE FROM BACKING

Carpet fibers usually do not separate from backing unless the carpet has been cleaned with improper products or has been allowed to remain wet for an extended period of time. Proper carpet maintenance is a Homeowner's Responsibility.

Resolution: Builder should deliver the finish floor in conformance with the above guidelines.

Recommendation: Do not clean carpet with improper products or allow it to remain wet for extended periods of time. Promptly clean any spills in accordance with the material manufacturer's recommendations.

FADING AND DISCOLORATION

Proper carpet maintenance is a Homeowner responsibility. Some amount of fading is unavoidable in areas that are exposed to sunlight. Spots are usually the result of spills or pet accidents. The Homeowner should promptly neutralize and remove any spills in a manner consistent with the manufacturer's recommendations.

Resolution: There should be no fades or discolorations at the time of the Walkthrough.

Recommendation: Choose carpet colors and types that will provide the longest life at sun-exposed locations. Do not let sunlight continuously beam onto carpet, as it may cause fading. Promptly clean any spills in accordance with the material manufacturer's recommendations.

PADDING MISSING UNDER PORTIONS OF THE CARPET

Carpet padding that is missing is unacceptable and should be added by the Builder. The exception to this is that some Builders choose to eliminate padding from closets that are not walk-in closets. This condition is acceptable in those areas.

Resolution: Builder should make the necessary repairs to meet the above guideline.

Recommendation: Homeowners should follow the manufacturer's cleaning and care instructions.

CARPET TEXTURE DOES NOT ALIGN AT SEAMS

Texture at seams should run in the same direction. Quarter turns are not acceptable.

Resolution: Builder should make the necessary repairs to meet the above Performance Guideline.

Recommendation: None. However, should follow the manufacturer's care and cleaning instructions.

CARPETS HAVE A DARK SOIL LINE AT STAIR AND BASEBOARD EDGES

Soil staining of carpets due to air infiltration can be reduced, but not eliminated at stair and baseboard edges. Builder should seal the plate behind the baseboard and stair edges with foam, caulk, or by making the joints tight.

Resolution: There should be no soil lines visible at the time of the Walkthrough.

Recommendation: Homeowner can expect some soiling to occur at baseboard and stair edges, even if the Builder has made a good faith effort to seal the edges. Homeowner should consider this when selecting carpet colors. Light colors can show edge marks in a short period of time.

THERE IS A BUMP AT THE TRANSITION BETWEEN CARPET AND HARD SURFACE FLOORING

There should be no more than 1/4-inch vertical displacement between different finish flooring surfaces. Ramping or floating the subfloor is an acceptable method to meet the Performance Guideline. Ramps should extend under the carpet at the rate of one foot horizontal for every 1/4-inch of vertical. Specifically designed transition strips, such as metal or wood, may be placed at the transition threshold to alert persons that they are stepping onto a different surface at a different level.

Resolution: Builder should perform appropriate repairs to satisfy the Guideline.

Recommendation: None.

PLASTER AND DRYWALL

DRYWALL / PLASTER IS CRACKED

Cracks in excess of 3/32-inch in width are considered unacceptable.

Resolution: Unless frame or foundation movement is causing significant cracking, the Builder should make necessary repairs to meet the above Performance Guideline. If frame or foundation movement is causing the cracking, this condition must first be remedied before attempting drywall or plaster repairs.

Recommendation: Cracks less than 3/32-inch in drywall and plaster are Homeowner maintenance items and may be patched with spackle or caulk.

DRYWALL HAS NAIL POPS

Nail pops that are visible from a distance of 6 feet under normal light conditions are unacceptable. Nail pops that have cracked the surface or with exposed heads are unacceptable. This guideline also applies to drywall screws.

Resolution: Builder shall make repairs as necessary to meet the above guideline.

Recommendation: None.

CORNER BEAD OR TAPE SEAM POPS

Cracked or pulled away corner beads, or tape seams that have pulled away and are visible from any angle at a distance of 6 feet under normal lighting conditions, are considered unacceptable.

Resolution: Builder shall make repairs as necessary to meet the above guideline.

Recommendation: None.

DRYWALL CROWNS IN CEILING, DRYWALL BOWS ON WALLS

Drywall crowns in ceilings should not exceed 1/4-inch in a 32-inch distance across. Drywall bows in walls should not exceed 3/16-inches in a 32-inch distance across.

Resolution: Builder should repair drywall crowns or bows in excess of the above guideline. Floating and retexturing is considered an acceptable repair method.

Recommendation: None. Measurement to determine compliance with this guideline, it should be made with a level or true straight edge tool no less than 6ft. in length.

SURFACE TEXTURE IS UNEVEN OR IRREGULAR

Textured surfaces should be consistent with the applicators intent; that is to say that texture that is designed to be knocked down should be reasonably uniform, and texture that is designed to be sprayed on without further treatment should be reasonably uniform throughout, when viewed from a distance of 6 feet under normal lighting conditions. Garages and other utility areas, which may be drywalled and textured, do not apply to this guideline for texture workmanship.

Resolution: If more than 10% of the wall surface contains dimples, blotches, tool marks or other irregularities when viewed at a distance of 6 feet under normal lighting conditions, the Builder should make repairs as necessary to provide a more uniform appearance.

Recommendation: The Homeowner should realize that wall and ceiling texturing is an art and not a precise science. Expect some irregularities. These irregularities are often more prominent at night when single light sources, such as light fixtures, cast shadows. Determining wall texture performance by feeling it is not an acceptable measure.

COUNTERTOPS

COUNTERTOP IS NOT LEVEL

Countertops should not exceed 1/4-inch of rise or drop in any 8-foot direction. Exception: certain tiles are made with an intentionally irregular, lumpy surface and these irregularities are acceptable.

Resolution: Builder should take corrective actions to level the countertop, including leveling the cabinets, if necessary.

Recommendation: None.

BACKSLASH IS LOOSE

Countertop backslashes should be tightly adhered to the wall

Resolution: Builder should make the corrections to repair the loose backsplash.

Recommendation: Cabinets expand and shrink with room moisture. Cracks will occur between the top and the splash. Homeowner should maintain the cracks with caulk or grout.

CERAMIC TILE COUNTERTOPS

UNEVEN SURFACE

Since there are a number of different types of ceramic tile, ranging from rough handmade varieties to the very precisely manufactured types, it is impractical to apply any one standard to all ceramic tiles. The general guideline for an entire countertop is no more than 1/8-inch of uneven surface in any direction in eight feet horizontally. For handmade tiles, the condition is established by using a long straightedge that rests on multiple high points along the countertop length. For very regular manufactured tiles, in addition to the level guideline, no point should occur more than 1/16-inch above or below a line parallel to the surface, and adjacent tiles should not be more than 1/32-inch out of level with each other.

Countertops can be totally level but should never slow away from drainage points such as sinks or basins.

Resolution: Builder should make repairs as necessary.

Recommendation: Always follow the manufacturer's care and cleaning recommendations for the specific ceramic tile.

UNEQUAL GROUT JOINTS

Different types of tiles call for grout joints of different widths. However, within any one area of tile (for precise and manufactured tiles), joints should not vary more than 1/32-inch from the widest to the narrowest.

Resolution: Builder should make repairs as necessary.

Recommendation: Always follow the manufacturer's care and cleaning recommendations for the specific ceramic tile

GROUT JOINT CRACKS

Hairline cracks may appear in grout joints where there are changes in the plane of the tile surface and where tile abuts a dissimilar material, such as at a backsplash or at a sink or wall. Excluding joints at changes in plane, cracks exceeding 5% of the total length of grout joint in any one-tile installation are considered non-performing.

Resolution: Builder should make repairs as necessary, provided the condition is not a result of inadequate Homeowner maintenance or misuse.

Recommendation: Homeowner should maintain caulking and repair incidental grout cracking, especially at backsplash and sink openings.

CRACKED TILE

Where cracks align across a number of consecutive tiles, the usual cause is movement of underlying building components. Isolated cracks in individual tiles may indicate Homeowner abuse of the countertop.

Resolution: If an underlying problem is identified after investigation, the Builder should make repairs as necessary.

Recommendation: Do not place unusually heavy objects on the tile surface; avoid dropping things on the tiles. Always follow the manufacturer's care and cleaning recommendations for the specific ceramic tile.

COLOR AND TEXTURE VARIATIONS

Tile used in any one area should be from the same batch, or lot, providing consistent appearance throughout. This does not apply to certain types of handmade tile in which variations are a desirable characteristic. Obvious changes in color and texture within a field of tile are not acceptable where the tile is intended to be of consistent appearance.

Resolution: Builder should make repairs as necessary.

Recommendation: Always follow the manufacturer's care and cleaning recommendations for the specific ceramic tile.

LOOSE TILE

Generally, tile should not come loose from the underlying surface to which it is applied. More specifically, tile can come loose as a result of improper original application of mortar, excessive deflection of the underlying material to which tile is applied or because of exposure to impact from heavy objects.

Resolution: If condition is a result of improper installation or construction and not a result of Homeowner misuse, Builder should make repairs as necessary.

Recommendation: Avoid dropping heavy objects on the tile surface. Always follow the manufacturer's care and cleaning recommendations for the specific ceramic tile.

WATER PENETRATION THROUGH TOP

Properly installed, countertops intended for use that involves exposure to significant amounts of water (food preparation areas, countertops adjacent to sinks and basins, etc.) should include a water resisting system adequate to prevent leaks through the countertop assembly.

Resolution: Builder should make repairs as necessary.

Recommendation: Always follow the manufacturer's care and cleaning recommendations for the specific ceramic tile

GRANITE, MARBLE, STONE COUNTERTOPS

CRACKS

Cracks in excess of 1/32-inch are considered non-performing. Cracks may be related to improper or inadequate installation, or a result of inadequate support. Improper use may also be a cause

Resolution: After investigation, Builder should repair or replace non-performing countertops as necessary; if the condition was not a result of improper use. Specialists in stone restoration should repair cracked marble, but before undertaking such repairs, the Builder should correct any underlying causes.

Recommendation: Maintain countertop in accordance with the recommendations of the material manufacturer and supplier. Maintain caulking and repair incidental grout cracking, especially at backsplash and sink openings. Do not drop heavy objects on countertops. Do not stand on countertop.

TEXTURE AND COLOR VARIATIONS

Countertops made up of multiple pieces should be assembled with reasonably well-matched colors. Severe variations in surface texture and color are unacceptable.

Resolution: Guideline should be met at the time of Home delivery.

Recommendation: While both texture and color are truly subjective in nature, a good rule of thumb is: If the Homeowner buys the House before the finish surfaces are set, the Homeowner should approve their placement. If the Homeowner buys the House after the finish surfaces are installed, the Homeowner accepts the finishes as installed.

STAINS

Granite marble and stone can be stained by a variety of products and natural materials, juices, etc. Protection of the surface is a Homeowner

Responsibility. Any pre-existing stains should be noted at the time of the Homeowner Walkthrough.

Resolution: Builder should correct any pre-existing stains noted at the Walkthrough. If pre-existing stains cannot be corrected, Builder should replace countertop.

Recommendation: Examine countertops carefully at the Walkthrough. Builders cannot be held responsible for this type of damage unless it is identified and disclosed at the time of the Walkthrough. Maintain countertop in accordance with the recommendations of the material manufacturer and supplier. Use only cleaning products approved by the manufacturer or the applicable trade association for the material. Do not use abrasives to clean any type of countertop. Avoid placing hot pots, pans, Crockpots, etc. in direct contact with the countertop.

CHIPS

Granite, marble, and stone countertops should not be delivered to the Homeowner scratched or chipped. Repairs of chips and scratches prior to the Walkthrough are acceptable provided the repair cannot be distinguished at a distance of six feet under normal lighting conditions. Chips on a top of any material should not penetrate more than 1/16-inch from the edge of the seam or grout joint, unless the manufacturing process intentionally created edge chips.

Resolution: Repair or replace countertops as necessary, provided that condition was not caused by Homeowner misuse or negligence.

Recommendation: Examine countertops carefully at the Walkthrough. Maintain countertop in accordance with the recommendations of the material manufacturer and supplier. Do not drop heavy objects on countertop.

PLASTIC LAMINATE COUNTERTOPS

OPEN JOINTS

A properly assembled plastic laminate countertop should have tight hairline joints without any openings where adjoining pieces meet. Joints that are separated by more than 1/32-inch are considered unacceptable and should be corrected by the Builder.

Resolution: Builder should repair or replace countertops as necessary, provided that condition was not caused by Homeowner misuse or negligence.

Recommendation: Examine countertops carefully at the Walkthrough. Maintain countertop in accordance with the recommendations of the material manufacturer and supplier.

DELAMINATION

Delamination occurs when the plastic laminate does not adhere to the underlayment. This is usually an adhesive application problem or curing problem. Edge strips are most commonly affected by this type of problem. Delamination is unacceptable and should be corrected by the Builder unless there is evidence of abusive use by the Homeowner.

Resolution: Builder should repair or replace countertops as necessary, provided that the condition was not caused by Homeowner misuse or negligence.

Recommendation: Maintain countertop in accordance with the recommendations of the material manufacturer and supplier. Maintain caulking, especially at backsplash and sink openings.

UNACCEPTABLE TRIMMING

Unacceptable trimming can include edges that are not straight and edges that are burned because of overheating of trimming cutters. Trimmed edges should be very straight and neat. The edge exposure area should be of a constant width throughout the countertop.

Resolution: Builder should repair or replace countertops as necessary.

Recommendation: Homeowner should maintain countertop in accordance with the recommendations of the material manufacturer and supplier.

STAINS AND BURNS

The countertop should be delivered to the Homeowner without stains, scratches, or burns.

Resolution: Builder should repair or replace any non-performing conditions noted at the time of the Walkthrough.

Recommendation: Examine countertops carefully at the Walkthrough. Builders cannot be held responsible for this type of damage unless it is identified and disclosed at the time of the Walkthrough. Maintain countertop in accordance with the recommendations of the material manufacturer and supplier. Use only cleaning products approved by the material manufacturer, never use abrasives. Avoid placing hot objects on countertops.

SOLID SURFACE COUNTERTOPS

OPEN SEAMS

Depending on the selected color and veining, there should be no conspicuous seams in the finished countertop. Proficient solid surface countertop installers are able to bond adjacent pieces so that the joint is virtually inconspicuous, but not necessarily invisible. Some solid surface pieces may be "soft-seamed" with a flexible silicone.

Resolution: Builder should repair or replace countertops as necessary.

Recommendation: Homeowner should examine countertops carefully at the Walkthrough. Maintain countertop in accordance with the recommendations of the material manufacturer and supplier.

ROUGHENED SURFACE

To finish solid surface countertops, it is necessary to sand the surface smooth. The resulting final surface should be smooth and consistent throughout. Surface texture variations that are clearly rough to the touch are considered unacceptable.

Resolution: Builder should repair or replace countertops as necessary, provided that condition was not caused by Homeowner misuse or negligence.

Recommendation: Homeowner should examine countertops carefully at the Walkthrough. Maintain countertop in accordance with the recommendations of the material manufacturer and supplier.

STAINS AND BURNS

There should be no stains or burns on any portion of the countertop at the time of the Homeowner Walkthrough.

Resolution: Builder should repair or replace any non-performing conditions noted at the Walkthrough.

Recommendation: Examine countertops carefully at the Walkthrough. Maintain countertop in accordance with the recommendations of the material manufacturer and supplier. Builders cannot be held responsible for this type of damage unless it is identified and disclosed at the time of the Walkthrough.

BLEMISHES AND SCRATCHES

A solid surface countertop is a product that is manufactured under closely controlled conditions. Therefore the countertop should be delivered to the Homeowner free of blemishes and scratches.

Resolution: Builder should repair or replace countertops as necessary.

Recommendation: Homeowner should examine countertops carefully at the Walkthrough. Maintain countertop in accordance with the recommendations of the material manufacturer and supplier. Builders cannot be held responsible for this type of damage unless it is identified and disclosed at the time of the Walkthrough.

CULTURE MARBLE COUNTERTOPS

The top and backsplash pieces should fit together without gaps. The installer is likely to caulk these joints with a compatible caulk. If there is a gap between the backsplash and the wall, this gap should also be caulked so that no gap is visible. No gap should be more than 1/4-inch wide, whether caulked or not.

Resolution: Builder should repair or replace countertops as necessary.

Recommendation: Examine countertops carefully at the Walkthrough. Maintain countertop in accordance with the recommendation of the material manufacturer and supplier.

BLEMISHES AND INCONSISTENT COLOR

Color swirls can vary significantly in cultured marble due to the fact that each batch is made like a marble cake. In general, the color swirls should be consistent throughout the top, and should not be concentrated in any one spot. The same guideline applies to any sparkles, if added to the mix.

Resolution: Builder shall repair or replace countertops as necessary.

Recommendation: Examine countertops carefully at the Walkthrough. Maintain countertop in accordance with the recommendation of the material manufacturer and supplier.

VOIDS AT SURFACE

There should be no voids (depressions) in the surface more than 1/32-inch in depth and no larger than one inch in diameter. There should be no more than four such voids in 8 square feet of surface.

Resolution: Repair or replace countertops as necessary, provided that condition was not caused by Homeowner misuse or negligence.

Recommendation: Examine countertops carefully at the Walkthrough. Maintain countertop in accordance with the recommendations of the material manufacturer and supplier. Do not drop heavy objects on countertop surfaces.

LEAKS AT JOINTS AND FITTINGS

All penetrations at the facets sink rims and back splashes should be watertight.

Resolution: Builder shall repair any unacceptable conditions.

Recommendation: Always maintain the countertop in accordance with the manufacturer's recommendations. If at any time Homeowner discovers product or installation problems, the Homeowner should notify the Builder promptly.

APPLIANCES

APPLIANCES DO NOT PERFORM AS INTENDED

All appliances should function in the manner that the manufacturer intended.

Resolution: Builder should repair the appliance in a prompt manner in accordance with the manufacturer's warranty.

Recommendation: Register all appliances with the manufacturer. Read and follow the manufacturer's operation instructions. Before making a service call, follow the Trouble Shooting Guide found in the appliance owner's manuals.

CABINETS AND VANITIES

CABINETS DESIGNED TO SET FLUSH WITH THE CEILING HAVE A VISIBLE GAP, SPACE, OR SEPARATION

Any space or gap along the top or sides of the cabinet frame that exceeds 3/16-inch is considered unacceptable.

Resolution: All cabinets should have the proper backing in the wall to support whatever product is being applied to that particular wall. If the cabinet or vanity does not meet the guideline and was not a result of negligence by the Homeowner, then the Builder should repair as necessary.

Recommendation: Homeowner should use caution when loading upper cabinets so as to not overload them. Heavy plates and dishes and canned goods do not belong in upper cabinets.

CABINETS ARE NOT SET *FLUSH* WITH ONE ANOTHER

The face (front) of a cabinet should not be more than 1/8 inch out of flat plane with connecting portions of other cabinet pieces. Corners should not be out of line more than 3/16 inches.

Resolution: If the cabinets do not meet the above Performance Guideline, then the Builder should repair or replace any non-performing cabinetry in order to satisfy the Guideline. When finishing or refinishing, Builder should attempt to match the original cabinetry.

Recommendation: The Homeowner should properly maintain all cabinets, particularly any cabinetry that is located in areas that are subject to moisture, i.e. kitchens, bathrooms or laundry rooms. Water should not be allowed to remain on any wood products, whether sealed or not. If it is determined that the Homeowner was negligent with maintenance, the Builder will not be held responsible.

CABINETS ARE WARPED

Cabinet doors should not warp more than ¼ inch from the face of the frame. If the door is flat, but the frame is warped, the same Performance Guideline applies.

Resolution: Any cabinet or cabinetry, including doors and drawer fronts, that do not meet the above Performance Guideline should be replaced either in part or in whole (assuming condition was not cause by Homeowner negligence). When finishing or refinishing, Builder should attempt to match the original cabinetry.

Recommendation: Cabinets, drawer fronts and doors need to be periodically inspected for excessive wear and/or deterioration of the finish.

CABINET DRAWER GUIDE HAS BROKEN

All doors and drawers should function smoothly and properly for their intended purpose.

Resolution: If a drawer or door does not meet the above guideline, then the Builder should repair or replace the portion of the cabinet that does not conform.

Recommendation: Homeowner should be careful not to overload the drawers. This puts additional stress on the guides, which could cause them to prematurely fail.

CABINET DRAWER IS BINDING DURING OPENING

Cabinet doors and drawers should open and close smoothly without tugging or pulling

Resolution: Builder should repair or replace the drawer or door that does not perform.

Recommendation: Homeowner should operate doors and drawers smoothly and easily. Do not overload the drawers. Metal drawer guides should be lubricated with light lubricating oil every two years.

CABINET DOOR SWING OPEN AND / OR WILL NOT STAY CLOSED

All door hinge mechanisms and catches should operate and function as intended. Whether closing or opening, the door should operate smoothly with reasonable ease or effort.

Resolution: Builder should repair or replace the drawer or door that does not meet the guideline.

Recommendation: Doors can go out of adjustment, depending upon the care and use that they have been put through. Do not slam, hang objects from, or pull on the door, as this will cause hinge mechanisms to weaken not only at their fastening points but also within the mechanisms themselves. Periodically inspect hinges and retighten if necessary.

DOORS OR DRAWERS HAVE CRACKS IN THE PANELS

Panel inserts in drawers and doors should not crack.

Resolution: Builder should replace cracked panels. An exact match of the wood grain or color cannot be expected.

Recommendation: Consider stained cabinets as furniture and treat the wood faces with furniture polish.

PLASTIC LAMINATE SURFACES ARE PEELING AWAY

Cabinets that are covered with high-pressure plastic laminate should not delaminate.

Resolution: If the cabinet delaminates and is not a result of negligence by the Homeowner, the Builder should make the repairs as necessary.

Recommendation: Proper care by the Homeowner is essential. Liquids should be cleaned up immediately and not left on a surface, particularly at joints or corners. This creates the potential for the breakdown of the glues used to laminate the surface to the substrate.

CABINETS DO NOT SIT LEVEL

Cabinets should not have a deviation of more than 3/8-inch out of level over 6 feet of length.

Resolution: Builder should make repairs as necessary. When finishing or refinishing, Builder should attempt to match the original cabinetry.

Recommendation: None.

CABINET DOORS DO NOT ALIGN WHEN CLOSED

Gaps between abutting doors should not exceed 1/8-inch.

Resolution: Builder should adjust doors to meet the guideline.

Recommendation: None.

CABINET FINISH (PAINT OR STAIN) IS IRREGULAR, MISMATCHED, OR BLOTCHY

Irregularities of wood color in stained cabinets are considered acceptable, unless two or more different stains were used. Painted cabinets should be uniform in color when viewed under normal lighting conditions at a distance of 6 feet.

Resolution: Builder should take corrective action to meet the above performance guideline.

Recommendation: None.

GAPS APPEAR BETWEEN SECTIONS WHERE CABINETS ARE JOINED

Gaps at the section where cabinet cases are joined that are in excess of 1/32-inch for painted cabinets and 1/16-inch for stained cabinets are considered unacceptable

Resolution: Builder should make repairs as necessary.

Recommendation: Be aware that painted cabinets will separate at the stiles due to normal drying out of the house frame. Bathroom and laundry fans should always be operating when those rooms are in use.

STAIN GRADE CABINETS SHOW A "DARK" BAND AROUND DOOR AND DRAWER OPENINGS

This condition can occur from the sun fading exposed areas of cabinetry.

Resolution: None.

Recommendation: If the Homeowner wants to achieve a uniform color, they can leave the doors and drawers slightly open and exposed to the light. This procedure may take up to a year to achieve a uniform result.

STAIRS AND RAILINGS

STAIRS HAVE GAPS BETWEEN TREADS, RISERS AND SKIRT BOARDS

Rough stairs that will receive a covering may have gaps up to 3/8-inch between stair components. Finish stairs shall not have gaps between components that are in excess of 3/32-inch.

Resolution: Builder shall make the necessary corrections within the warranty period. Filling gaps with a matching wood filler or hard wood putty is acceptable as long as the gap does not exceed 1/4-inch on rough stairs and 1/8-inch on finish stairs.

Recommendation: None.

STAIR TREADS AND RISERS ARE UNEVEN

The "run and rise" of stairs are set forth in the Building Code. Stair tread for residential construction is permitted to be no less than 10 inches deep. Risers are permitted to be no more than 7-3/4-inches high. Additionally, riser height from one tread to the next cannot vary by more than 3/8-inch and the tread depth cannot vary by more than 3/8-inch from one tread to the next.

Resolution: Builder shall make adjustments in the staircase to meet the Code.

Recommendation: None.

STAIR TREAD DEFLECTS EXCESSIVELY

Stair tread deflection shall not exceed 1/8-inch under 200 pounds of vertically applied pressure.

Resolution: Builder shall reinforce the stair frame as needed. If the deflection is due to an overcut support, it may be sufficient to shim the support to stop the deflection. If shim is required on the concrete side of the framing, remember, wood in contact with concrete shall be pressure treated.

Recommendation: None.

STAIR TREADS SQUEAK

Wooden stairs should not squeak excessively

Resolution: Depending upon the terms of the warranty, Builder shall make a good faith attempt to eliminate or reduce excessively squeaking stairs.

Recommendation: Be aware that even the most perfectly build wooden staircase may develop some squeaks.

STAIR RAILINGS DEFLECT EXCESSIVELY

Deflection of stair railings shall be within tolerances of the Building Code.

Resolution: Builder shall secure guardrails and stair railings to meet the tolerance of the Code.

Recommendation: Homeowners have a duty to take care of guardrails and stair rails, and do not do anything that would cause them to become loose from their anchor points. This would include children playing on railings, or several adults consistently leaning on deck rails to exceed the 200-pound limit.

MOLDINGS AND TRIM

GAPS APPEAR AT JOINTS

No separation should exceed 1/16-inch in width at the time the house is delivered to the new Homeowner.

Resolution: If the gaps or splits are greater than the standard at time of delivery, the Builder should make the necessary repairs as needed. When finishing or refinishing, Builder should attempt to match the original material.

Recommendation: During the first year of the life of the house, the framing lumber will shrink. This action is likely to cause some gaps in trim and molding. If the gaps are less than that of the guideline, the Homeowner should putty and/or caulk, and sand and refinish in order to prevent any further splitting or separation to the molding or trim.

NAIL HEADS ARE VISIBLE IN THE FINISHED WOODWORK

Finish nails or staples should be set below the surface; holes should be filled and finished. If finish nail holes are visible from a distance of 6 feet under normal light (daylight), this is unacceptable.

Resolution: Builder should make the necessary repairs, as necessary. When finishing or refinishing, Builder should attempt to match the original materials.

Recommendation: None.

GAPS OCCUR WHERE MOLDING ABUTS ONE ANOTHER OR ABUTS ANOTHER MATERIAL

No separation should exceed 1/16-inch in width at the time the house is delivered to the Homeowner.

Resolution: Builder should make the necessary repairs to meet any deficiency. When finishing or refinishing, Builder should attempt to match the original materials.

Recommendation: If the gaps are within the guideline, Homeowner should putty and/or caulk, sand and refinish in order to prevent any further splitting or separation to the molding or trim.

MOLDING OR TRIM IS SPLIT OR CHECKED

All finished woodwork should be smooth and without any surface marks at the time of the Walkthrough. Caulking or filling gaps is acceptable, as long as the filled area blends in with the surrounding surface when viewed from a distance of 6 feet under normal lighting conditions (daylight).

Resolution: If the subject woodwork does not meet the guideline at the time of the Walkthrough, then the Builder should correct it by replacing and/or filling, puttying, sanding and refinishing as necessary to meet the guideline. When finishing or refinishing, Builder should attempt to match the original materials.

Recommendation: Depending on the climate/environment, wood products, even interior woods, may need more than normal maintenance. If cracks occur, it is important to seal these cracks by either caulking or puttying, then sanding and refinishing. This is very important in order to prevent any moisture from migrating to the unprotected backside of the wood, potentially causing twisting and warping.

HAMMER MARKS OR OTHER MARRS ARE VISIBLE

Hammerhead marks or other marks should not be visible from a distance of 6 feet under normal light conditions (daylight).

Resolution: Builder should make all repairs, as necessary. When finishing or refinishing, Builder should attempt to match the original materials and colors.

Recommendation: Homeowner should inspect all trim and molding work during the Walkthrough.

MIRRORS

SCRATCHES ON GLASS SURFACE

If scratches or imperfections are visible under normal lighting conditions and are noticeable from a distance of 3 feet or more, the mirror is considered non-performing (providing the glass was not damaged as a result of any Homeowner negligence).

Resolution: If the mirror does not meet the guideline, then the Builder should replace the mirror.

Recommendation: The Homeowner should thoroughly inspect all mirrors for any irregularities within the glazing at the time of the Walkthrough.

MIRROR BACKING IS DETERIORATING

When viewing the mirror from the front, there should be no visible imperfections, peeling, flaking and/or discoloration within the metallic backing material of the mirror.

Resolution: Builder should replace any mirror that does not conform to the guideline.

Recommendation: Homeowner should thoroughly inspect all mirrors for any irregularities within the glazing and its metallic backing at the time of the walkthrough. When cleaning a mirror, use caution when using cleaners that contain ammonia or vinegar. Ammonia and vinegar are excellent glass cleaners, however they can be extremely damaging to the metallic backing of the mirror. Also, do not allow cleaners to go over the top, sides or to get into the track at the bottom of the mirror. Manufacturers often recommended applying cleaning agents to a cloth, and then wiping down the mirror.

MIRROR WARDROBE DOORS DO NOT HAVE SAFETY BACKING (WALK-IN CLOSETS)

Mirror wardrobe doors used as the entry to walk-in closets should have safety backing with labels stating that they have met the following standards: ANSI Z97

Resolution: Builder should replace all mirror doors used on walk-in closets and do not meet this standard.

Recommendation: None.

SHOWER AND TUB ENCLOSURES

GLASS/PLASTIC IS SCRATCHED

At the time of delivery of the House, shower and tub enclosure glass or plastic panels should not be scratched.

Resolution: Builder should replace any glass or plastic panels that are scratched at the time of the Walkthrough.

Recommendation: Be aware that any claims for scratched shower and tub enclosure panels may not be honored by the Builder after the walkthrough.

SHOWER OR TUB ENCLOSURES LEAK

Shower doors should not leak through the frame. Shower enclosures should not leak through the joint between the door edge and the frame, or at the door bottom.

Resolution: Builder should make necessary repairs so there is no leakage at the enclosures frame (this excludes the intersection of the two movable panels on a tub enclosure). If there is leakage at the shower enclosure door, determine if it is improper installation or Homeowner caused by directing the showerhead at the door opening while showering.

Recommendation: Become aware of the proper use of a tub and shower enclosure. Keep shower water directed away from the door and panels. Continuous leaking may result in rot of the underlayment and subfloor. Continuous leaking also creates an environment for mold and mildew growth and for termites. The enclosure track should never be used as a handle to pull a bather up into a standing position.

FIBERGLASS OR ACRYLIC TUB BOTTOM OR SHOWER STALL ENCLOSURE FLEXES WHEN OCCUPIED

Some flexing of tub and shower sidewalls and bases is permissible, as long as the installation conforms to the manufacturer's guidelines.

Resolution: If the tub or shower has been installed in accordance with the manufacturer's instructions, the Builder does not have any responsibility. If the tub or shower has not been installed per the manufacturer's installation instructions, Builder shall make necessary repairs to conform the manufacturer's instructions.

Recommendation: Homeowner has a duty to learn the care and maintenance of synthetic bath surfaces, and shall notify Builder if the fitting cracks or pulls away from its supports.

SHOWER/TUB ENCLOSURES ARE NOT TEMPERED GLASS

If glass is used in shower and tub enclosures, it must be tempered. If plastic panels are used, they must be approved by the local Building Official.

Resolution: Unless approved plastic is used in shower and tub enclosures, all glass panels should be tempered.

Recommendation: None.

TOP RAIL OF SHOWER/TUB ENVLOSURE IS NOT SCREWED TO THE FRAME

The top rail of a tub or shower enclosure should be screwed to the frame or mechanically connected in a manner approved by the local Building Official.

Resolution: The Builder should take the necessary corrective measures to conform to the above requirement.

Recommendation: None.

GROUT IS CRACKED BETWEEN THE TUB/SHOWER AND FIRST ROW OF TILE

The grout should not be cracked at the bottom of the first course of tile at the time of Walkthrough (hairline cracks are expected.)

Resolution: Builder shall make repairs as necessary if grout cracks are noted at Walkthrough.

Recommendation: Tile grout should be sealed by the Homeowner prior to use; with a silicone-based sealer that can be purchased at any hardware store. Grout should be cleaned frequently and should be kept free of mold and mildew. When significant cracking first appears, the gout joint between the bottom row of tile and the top of the shower floor or tub should be caulked with a caulking compound made for bathroom use. Many grout manufacturers also make flexible sealants, both standard and smooth, to match their grout colors. Old caulk or grout should be dug out and discarded; new caulk should not be applied over old caulk.

WATER RESISTANT BACKING IMPROPERLY INSTALLED AT TUB OR SHOWER SURROUNDINGS

If backing is to be used at tub and shower surrounds, it must be water-resistant. Materials such as cement board or special water resistant paper may be used. However, lath and mortar are preferred. Water-resistant gypsum board is a Code-permitted alternative.

Resolution: Builder should use an appropriate water-resistant backing material at tub and shower surrounds and water-resistant drywall at other potentially damps locations.

Recommendation: Make certain that a coat of premium enamel paint is maintained on the drywall surface in. Maintain the caulking between the tubs or shower pan and the first row of tile.

UTILITY SYSTEMS

HEATING

SOME ROOMS ARE COMFORTABLE, WHILE OTHER ROOMS ARE COLD

The heating system should be designed so that every room that is supposed to be heated achieves a temperature of 68 degrees F when the temperature of the house has stabilized. All measurements should be made in the middle of the room, three feet up from the floor and two feet from exterior walls, or according to local energy standards. A temperature variation of 4 degrees F from room-to-room is considered acceptable, and the fan switch on the thermostat can be set to "fan on" to increase circulation and reduce room-to-room temperature differences.

Resolution: Builder should design and balance the heating system so that the above referenced guideline is met. If Homeowner has failed to cover large window openings so as to minimize heat loss, or has blocked the system's airflow in any manner, Builder should not be responsible.

Recommendation: Homeowner should be aware that it is not possible to achieve a uniform temperature throughout the house. A difference in temperature will also exist between the thermostat location and other rooms, particularly if those rooms are located above or below the thermostat location. Large window areas should be properly draped or otherwise protected from heat loss, and no furniture or other devices should be placed in rooms so as to impede the airflow. Most air supply grills (registers) have dampers that can be adjusted in rooms for difference in the summer and winter temperature needs. Homeowner should change or clean the furnace filter pursuant to the manufacturer's recommendations (usually no less than every six months). A dirty filter will reduce airflow and cause the system to use more energy.

THERMOSTAT DOES NOT WORK

Thermostat should perform as designed throughout its useful life. The thermostat can vary 4 degrees F from actual room temperature without being considered unacceptable.

Resolution: Builder should replace non-performing thermostat, assuming that the condition is not resulting from Homeowner negligence or failure to change the batteries.

Recommendation: Check thermostat periodically and change the batteries when it is indicated that batteries are weak. Do not leave dead batteries in a thermostat, especially during months when the system is not being used. Dead batteries can leak and corrode the thermostat.

SYSTEM IS NOISY WHEN OPERATING

Noise levels in bedrooms should not exceed 25dB (decibels) and noise levels in other rooms should not exceed 40dB.

Resolution: Builder should control noise levels in the cooling and heating system in conformance with the above standard. Further, if part of the system is loose internally and rattles as the system is operating, Builder should make adjustments to remove the rattling noise. Systems mounted in attics should be isolated from frame members.

Recommendation: Keep all air supply registers open to avoid noisy whistling sounds.

HEATING SYSTEM MAKES BOOMING NOISE WHEN FIRST TURNED ON, OR WHEN COOLING DOWN

It may not be possible to completely eliminate the noise from this effect.

Resolution: Builder should make all attempts to minimize this effect.

Recommendation: None.

HEATING SYSTEM MAKES BOOMING NOISE WHEN FIRST TURNED ON

All furnace burners should ignite quickly and smoothly as designed, without delay, and should not permit excessive accumulation of unburned fuel gases. The time for burner ignition should be no more than 15 seconds, and the startup time for the furnace blower should be 45 to 120 seconds after burner ignition.

Resolution: Builder should make appropriate adjustments to the burner ignition device.

Recommendation: If a booming noise is head when the furnace is turned on, the Homeowner has a duty to notify the Builder of this condition. The furnace should be maintained annually, and if any problems are observed with burner ignition or blower start up, the Builder should be notified during the warranty period, and a qualified heating and cooling contractor or the local gas utility company should be notified thereafter.

COLD SPOTS DEVELOP ON THE FLOOR (RADIANT SYSTEM)

Radiant heating systems should not leak or become clogged during their useful life.

Resolution: Builder should make the necessary repairs to assure the system provides continuous and uniform heat. However, beyond the initial charging of the system, Builder should not be responsible when approved fluids are added (such as hard water that may be used to recharge to system).

Recommendation: A radiant heating system requires little maintenance, but if make-up fluid constantly needs to be added to the system, there may be a leak. Leaks should be reported to the Builder immediately, since they can cause the soil to swell and undermine the slab, etc.

DUCT WORK HAS SEPARATED

Ductwork should be continuous and should not have gaps, breaks, or holes. Ducts should be sealed tight.

Resolution: Builder should secure and repair all separated duct work and repair any holes, provided that the unacceptable condition was not caused by the Homeowner or by a someone hired by the Homeowner (such as cable installer, alarm installer, termite inspector, etc.).

Recommendation: Homeowner should be aware that after contractors who install alarm systems or pest control companies, etc. have well-deserved reputations for tearing and squashing ductwork in attics and crawl spaces. If the Homeowner is having work done of this nature, he or she should inspect the crawl space or attic both prior to and after the work is done, to ensure that all ductwork remains intact.

COOLING

AIR CONDITIONER DOES NOT COOL THE HOUSE

Central air conditioning shall be capable of meeting the system design temperature. Typically this is a maximum difference between outside and inside temperatures of 20 degrees. To provide an accurate measurement of this differential, the air conditioning system must have been operating for 12 hours.

Resolution: If the air conditioning system does not meet the design and performance requirements of the local Energy Standards, Builder shall repair or replace the system so that it meets the performance criteria of such.

Recommendation: The "Away Setting on your thermostat should be no more than 4 degrees F higher than the "return" setting. Turning the system off when you go to work and then on when you return is not likely to achieve the desired temperature by bedtime; your system is designed to operate continuously. Repeated on-and-off cycles do not remove the humidity from the house and result in higher energy costs; All windows and sliding glass doors, particularly those facing south and west, should have insulating drapes or shades that are closed during the hottest times of the day; Sunrooms, solariums and similar spaces that gather light also gather heat. These areas should be separated from the rest of the house by doors that block heat from moving into the main rooms of the house; and Do not place any tinting material on the inside pane of the dual pane windows. This can cause excessive heat buildup between the panes of glass and result in rupture of the seals between the two layers of glass. Also, it is likely to void the warranty provided by the window manufacturer.

SOME ROOMS ARE HOTTER (OR COLDER) THAN OTHERS

A temperature variation of 4 degrees F from one room to another is considered acceptable. In two story houses, a temperature variation of 8 degrees F between the first and second floor is considered acceptable.

Resolution: The system should be balanced to meet the above standard.

Recommendation: For a more uniform cooling (and heating) between rooms and floors turn the fan switch on the thermostat from Auto to On.

RERIGERANT LINES LEAK

Refrigerant lines should not leak. They are part of closed loop system.

Resolution: Builder should repair the leak and recharge the system, assuming the Homeowner or Homeowner's contractor did not cause the leak.

Recommendation: Homeowners should prevent children from playing around air conditioning condensers. They should also maintain the manufacturer's recommended clearance between the condenser and any landscaping, fencing, or other structures. Refer to the manufacturer's warranty and the annual maintenance requirements. Do not move, raise, lower, or relocated condenser, doing so may void the units warranty.

CONDENSATE LINE IS PLUGGED

This is a Homeowner maintenance item.

Resolution: None.

Recommendation: Condensate lines should be inspected twice a year: at the beginning of the air conditioning season and at the end. If a trickle discharge is reduced to an occasional drip, it potentially means that the condensate line is in the process of becoming plugged. Another symptom of a plugged condensate line is cold-water droplets blowing out of the air supply grills in the house. If water is observed dripping from a pipe over the front of a window or patio door, or onto a garage floor, it is likely that the primary condensate line is plugged. If this occurs, shut off the air conditioner and schedule the system for servicing.

COMPRESSOR FAILS

Compressor should not fail within the manufacturer's warranty period

Resolution: Builder shall replace the failed compressor if it fails within the warranty period.

Recommendation: None.

SYSTEM FAILS TO TURN ON WHEN FIRST ACTIVATED IN SPRING/SUMMER

Air conditioning systems should turn on as intended. This is a Homeowner maintenance item.

Resolution: None.

Recommendation: Once every two months, on warm winter days, the air conditioner should be started and run for a few minutes to keep the internal parts clean and lubricated.

COMPRESSOR UNIT IS OUT OF LEVEL

Compressor units should be set level to a tolerance of 1 inch in any direction, unless otherwise stated by the manufacturer

Resolution: Builder should set the compressor unit to meet the above guideline at the time of the Walkthrough and during the warranty period.

Recommendation: Moving the unit may void the warranty.

EVAPORATIVE COOLER BLOWS WARM AIR

Evaporative coolers should not blow air that is the same temperature as the outside air. The cooler should provide cool air in accordance with the manufacturer's specifications.

Resolution: If the evaporative cooler does not meet the manufacturer's performance specifications, the Builder should repair or replace the non-performing cooler. The Builder is not responsible for service problems due to poor water quality.

Recommendation: Evaporative coolers need to be kept clean and free of mineral build-up in order to operate properly. Depending upon local water quality, evaporative coolers need to be treated and backwashed periodically.

ELECTRICAL

LIGHTS FLICKER WHEN APPLIANCES ARE TURNED ON

If the circuit is not overloaded by the Homeowner, and if lightly flicker continuously and the breaker do not trip, the circuit is unacceptable.

Resolution: The Builder should inspect the circuit, determine the problem, and make the necessary repairs. The Builder is not responsible for momentary flickering when high capacity appliances are plugged into wall outlets.

Recommendation: Avoid overloading circuits with multiple appliances and add-on outlets. If wires feel warm to the touch, they should be unplugged and reinserted into a separate circuit. Note: Circuit breakers are found in the main panel where the meter is located or in the subpanel. The circuits should be labeled inside the panels.

BREAKERS TRIP OR FUSES BLOW FREQUENCY

Circuit breakers that trip frequently and fuses that blow frequently, under proper design usage, are indications of an unacceptable circuit or a malfunctioning appliance.

Resolution: Builder should test circuits to determine their capacity and make necessary corrections if the circuits are found to be inadequate for expected normal usage by the Homeowner.

Recommendation: Homeowner should not overload circuits to the point where fuses blow or breakers trip. If frequent tripping occurs, the Homeowner has a duty to notify the Builder. **DO NOT replace a fuse or circuit breaker with one that has a higher rating or one made by a different manufacturer! This action could result in a fire.**

GROUND FAULT INTERRUPTER TRIPS FREQUENTLY

Ground fault interrupters should be installed in accordance with the National Electric Code or other applicable Code in effect at the time.

Resolution: None, assuming the installation was done pursuant to the applicable Code and that the GFI device itself is acceptable.

Recommendation: Test GFIs monthly by pressing the black test button. Do not plug a freezer or refrigerator into a GFI outlet.

ALUMINUM WIRE, NOT COPPER WIRE, WAS INSTALLED

House wiring should be installed per applicable Code.

Resolution: Builder should install wiring per applicable Code.

Recommendation: None.

LIGHT FIXTURES TARNISH

Light fixtures should not be tarnished at time of delivery of House.

Resolution: Builder shall repair or replace fixtures that do not conform at time of delivery of the House.

Recommendation: Inspect fixtures during the Walkthrough. Check with fixture manufacturers regarding their warranty. Fixtures, especially bright brass, will need to be cleaned and polished as routine maintenance.

LIGHT SWITCHES AND OUTLET PLATES PROTRUDE TOO FAR FROM WALL

Switch and plug plates that protrude more than 1/16-inch from the finished wall are considered unacceptable.

Resolution: Builder should adjust switch and outlet plates to be flush and level in the wall. For minor protrusions less than 1/16-inch, caulking in an acceptable repair.

Recommendation: None.

LIGHT SWITCHES STICK OR MUST BE JIGGLED TO TURN THE LIGHT ON

Light switches that stick or require tapping or jiggling to turn on lights or appliance are unacceptable.

Resolution: Builder should replace all light switches that operate in a non-performing manner

Recommendation: None.

WALL OUTLET IN BEDROOM DOES NOT WORK

A bedroom must have an overhead light or a wall outlet that is turned on from a switch by the door.

Resolution: None, assuming that the outlet is properly switched.

Recommendation: The wall outlet (also known as a "half hot", and is typically installed upside down to identify it) is controlled by the light switch. Flip the light switch on and the outlet should operate.

BATHROOM FANS / LAUNDRY FANS ARE NOISY

These fans can be noisy. This is not a condition of non-performance unless the sound is a result of fan blades hitting part of the housing unit.

Resolution: Unless the fan blades are hitting the housing or other solid object, Builder has no responsibility.

Recommendation: Do not disconnect the bath or laundry fans because they create an annoying noise. Moist air must be exhausted to the outside; otherwise mold and mildew can form on the walls and ceiling. Fans should be operated while these rooms are in use.

PLUMBING

WATER OR GAS PIPING LEAKS

Water supply piping, gas piping, wastewater piping, and fire sprinkler plumbing should not leak. Piping must contain and convey 100% of the liquid or gas that it is intended to convey.

Resolution: Builder should make corrective repairs to any leaking piping system. Builder is not responsible for piping leaks caused by earthquakes or shifts in the structure that were not caused by Builder.

Recommendation: The Homeowner has a duty to notify the Builder upon noticing any gas or liquid leaks in piping, no matter how small. Failure to give timely notice can result in health hazards, personal injury, and structural damage, etc. Homeowner should have the fire sprinkler system professionally tested annually (or more frequently if required by the local fire authorities) to determine that the system will operate as designed in the event of a fire.

WATER PIPES FREEZE

In geographic areas where freezing weather is normal, water supply and waste piping should be protected from freezing. For geographic areas where freezing weather is rare, unprotected pipes are considered acceptable.

Resolution: Protect all pipes from freezing weather if the House is constructed in an areas where freezing weather is normal and customary. If the Homeowner does not maintain minimum heat, the Builder is not responsible for any leaking pipes due to freezing that occurs in any portion of the House that is intended to be heated.

Recommendation: To protect against the nuisance of infrequent freezing weather, the Homeowner can at his or her option purchase protective materials such as pipe insulation and electric resistant heat tape at any local hardware store. If the Homeowner is going to be gone for a period of time during possible freezing weather, the thermostat should be set on "heat" at its minimum setting.

WATER TASTES FUNNY, SMELLS, OR IS DISCOLORED

Water should be of good quality. However, the Builder may not have control over the quality of water supplied by the local water district.

Resolution: None, unless the Builder is responsible for creating the water supply to the house. This does not mean installing the water piping system that is to be taken over by a municipal authority. If the Builder is responsible for supplying the source of water, the Builder, should provide water that meets minimum quality standards as set by the governing agency, such as the local County Department of Health or the State of California Department of Water Quality. The Builder should not be responsible for changes in water quality once the quality meets the local or State set standards. For example, a change in nearby agricultural uses, or mining activity subsequent to construction, may cause changes in water quality that are not the Builders Responsibility.

Recommendation: If water quality standards are met by the Builder and/or the local water supply agency, and are still unacceptable to the

Homeowner, consider a whole house filtration system or use of a drinking water service company.

TOLIET BACKS UP, DRAINS BACK UP

At the time of the Walkthrough, all fixtures should operate as intended and all drains should flow freely.

Resolution: Builder is not responsible for post-Walkthrough conditions, unless it can be determined that the cause of the blockage was from construction related activity.

Recommendation: Sink, tub, and shower traps should be kept free and clear as routine maintenance items. Material such as hair, toothpaste, sanitary napkins, etc. may accumulate in the traps and could eventually cause a backup. Try to keep these materials from getting into the trap in the first place, and use a drain cleaner every 3-4 months to keep the traps scoured out and free from debris build-up. Learn the proper use of a low-flush toilet.

INADEQUATE WATER PRESSURE

For houses that are connected to the municipal water system or mutual water system of 10 houses or more, the house piping system should be designed to operate between pressures of 15psi and 80psi. For houses that are connected to a well or a mutual water system of 10 houses or fewer, the water pressure should be subject to the capacity of the well and the output of its equipment.

Resolution: Provided the Builder has met the local Code for water pipe system sizing, the Builder has no responsibility.

Recommendation: In areas where the water service is at the lower end of the allowable pressure range, water flows from fixtures will be less. This condition is beyond the control of the Builder and should be addressed with the agency that supplies that water. If the problem persists, consider installing a booster pump to increase pressure. Using several fixtures simultaneously may also result in low water flow and decrease in pressure.

SEWER GAS SMELL COMING FROM DRAIN

This is a homeowner maintenance item unless the sewer gas is coming from a cracked pipe

Resolution: None.

Recommendation: Sewer gas smells coming from drains typically indicate a lack of water in the trap. This occurs when a drain is not used for long periods of time and the water evaporates from the trap. Pouring a large glass of water in the drain will fill the trap sufficiently.

COPPER WATER PIPES OR BLACK GAS PIPES ARE WET ON THE OUTSIDE

Condensation on the outside of water lines is normal condition

Resolution: Builder should install pipe insulation on cold water pipes where there is a likelihood of condensation and mold growth.

Recommendation: None.

FAUCETS DRIP

At the time of the Walkthrough, all washers and cartridges should seat tightly and faucets should not leak.

Resolution: Any faucets that leak at the time of the Walkthrough should be repaired.

Recommendation: Washers and cartridges should be replaced at the time when dripping is first noticed. Many cartridges have a 5-year to lifetime guarantee on parts. Most of the current bathroom and kitchen faucets are made with cartridges and require only infrequent replacement. Hose bibs (the valves that a hose is connected to on the outside of the House) are made with washers. Depending upon the amount of use, hose bib washers may need to be replaced as frequently as every six months or as infrequently as every 3 years. If leaking occurs at the "stem" or handle of the valve (often at the hose bib or water heater), the nut at the base of the stem can be tightened or repacked to solve this problem.

SINK/TUB IS CHIPPED

Fixtures should not be chipped at time of delivery. Chips, mars, or discolorations 1/32-inch or less are considered acceptable

Resolution: Builder shall repair any chips, mars, or discolorations that exceed the above standard that are observed at the time of the Walkthrough.

Recommendation: None.

SHOWER HEAD PIPE/TUB SPOUT IS LOOSE

At time of delivery, showerhead pipes and tub spouts should be secured so they cannot move in or out more than 1/4-inch

Resolution: Non-conforming conditions shall be cured when noted at time of the Walkthrough.

Recommendation: Avoid hanging heavy objects such as shower caddies full of bating shampoos and lotions on the showerhead pipe.

FIBERGLASS TUB/SHOWER FLEXES WHEN OCCUPIED

Fiberglass and acrylic tub and shower units should be installed in accordance with the manufacturer's instructions.

Resolution: If installation is not made in accordance with the manufacturer's instructions, Builder should correct the non-performing condition.

Recommendation: None.

WATER DRAINS FROM SINK/TUB WHEN STOPPED IS ENGAGED

Water should not drain past the stopper mechanism at a rate of which the depth of water in the sink or tub decreases by more than one-inch per hour.

Resolution: Sinks and tubs which drain more quickly than permitted under the guideline, and whose stoppers have been properly maintained, should be adjusted or replaced as necessary.

Recommendation: Periodic cleaning and maintenance of mechanical sink and tub stoppers is a Homeowner responsibility. Stoppers should be checked monthly.

BRASS BATHROOM FAUCETS AND DRAINS TARNISH

Brass fittings should be free from tarnish at the time of delivery; brass fittings that become tarnished subsequent to the Walkthrough are acceptable.

Resolution: Builder shall replace any brass fittings on bathroom fixtures that are tarnished at the time of the Walkthrough.

Recommendation: Brass is beautiful but "soft" metal. It is easily scratched and tarnished. Follow the manufacturer's instructions when cleaning brass. Cleansers with abrasives and cleansers with ammonia are likely to scratch and chemically attack brass finishes. Wipe brass finishes frequently.

TOLIET RUNS CONTINUOUSLY

When a toilet tank fills, it should shut off. Water should not run continuously through the overflow pipe or flapper valve.

Resolution: Builder should make corrections to toilet tank system so that the water shuts off when the tank is filled to the appropriate level.

Recommendation: Toilet tanks have mechanical parts inside them and these parts wear out over time. Depending upon the amount of use and water quality, replacing worn flappers, floats, and valves can occur as frequently as once a year or as infrequently as every 10 years. Water supplies with higher concentrations of minerals (known as hard water) will leave deposits inside the toilet tank and its parts. This condition will cause more frequent replacement and rebuilding of toilet parts than those areas that do not have high mineral content in the water supply.

TOLIET LEAKS AT FLOOR

Toilets should not leak at the floor

Resolution: Builder should make necessary repairs to ensure a watertight flow between the toilet and the House waste plumbing.

Recommendation: The Homeowner has the duty to notify the Builder of any leaking toilet before additional damage occurs. Toilets that are permitted to leak will cause structural damage if the toilet is located over a wood subfloor. A toilet that leaks creates a condition for termites to enter the House, regardless of whether it sits on a wooden subfloor or a slab.

Termites are attracted to dark, damp conditions in the soil. It is important to note that a toilet that rocks back and forth or moves side to side may be leaking, even though no leak is visible. The Homeowner has a duty to notify the Builder of this condition.

LACK OF HOT WATER

Builder should provide a hot water system, either gas or electric, that supplies hot water to all appropriate fixtures in the House. Some Energy Codes do not require that all hot water pipes that pass through unheated spaces (such as garages, crawl spaces, and attics) should be insulated provided that the Builder has installed other energy conserving devices that make the entire House code complaint. See your local code requirement for specific requirements.

Resolution: If the above Standard is not met, Builder should take corrective measures so that it is met.

Recommendation: Frequent demand over short time periods (such as morning showers by an entire family) can result in a lack of hot water until the water heater has had time to recover; this is not a Builder responsibility. If the Homeowner wishes to increase water temperature, he or she can adjust the control dial on most water heaters. Electric water heaters are often pre-set and cannot be adjusted. However, it is very important to recognize that the higher the temperature setting, the greater the danger of scalding. **CAUTION!** Before entering the tub or shower, always turn on water and adjust it to a safe and proper temperature. Children, elderly people (or any person), should never be placed in a tub or shower before the water is turned on and the temperature safely adjusted. Although many of the gas water heaters today have automatic ignition systems, the Homeowner should become familiar with how to manually light a water heater pilot.

WATER HEATER IS NOT EARTHQUAKE SECURED, AS REQUIRED

Water heater should be strapped or secured in Code approved manner to prevent tip-over during an earthquake.

Resolution: If the water heater is not strapped or secured to the frame of the House in a manner prescribed by Code, Builder should take the proper corrective measures.

Recommendation: None.

ELECTRIC WATER HEATER CIRCUIT BREAKER TRIPS CONTINUOUSLY

Electric water heater breakers should not trip. Tripping is an indication of an electrical problem within the heater or the wiring to the heater.

Resolution: Builder should take corrective measures to eliminate electrical water heater breaker tripping.

Recommendation: As electric water heaters age, their heating element can wear out and fall to the bottom of the tank. If this condition occurs, the circuit breaker cannot be reset, and the Homeowner needs to replace the water heater.

FIRE SPRINKLER SYSTEM

FIRE SPRINKLER PIPES OR FITTINGS LEAK

Fire sprinkler systems should not leak

Resolution: Builder shall repair leaking pipes, fittings, etc. as required to eliminate leaks.

Recommendation: Do not paint any fire sprinkler heads or covers or hand any objects from the head. Be aware that if the drywall is removed from the ceiling, such as in repair or remodel, plastic sprinkler pipes could melt because they would be exposed directly to a fire.

SPRINKLER HEADS AND ESCUTCHEONS DO NOT FIT FLUSH TO WALL, OR ARE OUT OF LINE WITH DRYWALL OPENINGS

All sprinkler heads and their escutcheons should fit neatly and tightly to wall and ceiling finishes. Escutcheons should not protrude more than 1/8-inch as measured from the back of the plate beyond the wall surface.

Resolution: Installation should conform to the Performance Guideline. Builder should correct any sprinkler heads that are out of line or do not fit neatly to finish surfaces.

Recommendation: None.

TELEPHONE

NO DIAL TONE, OR STATIC SOUNDS ARE HEARD

A clear signal (dial tone) should be provided from the interface to all jacks within the House. The maximum signal loss between the interface and any jack should not exceed 6dB.

Resolution: If the telephone service provider identifies the problem as being on the house side of the interface, the Builder should remediate the deficiency.

Recommendation: The addition of "after-market" alterations to the house telephone system may affect the performance of the original wiring.

CABLE TV

TV RECEPTION IS SNOWY, WAVEY OR OTHERWISE UNCLEAR

If the CATV wiring within the House is installed by the Builder, there should be a clear, uninterrupted signal to each outlet, with a maximum signal loss of 8 dB between the interface and any one outlet.

Resolution: Upon report of a problem by Homeowner and a statement by the CATV provider that the problem is on the house side of the interface, Builder should take corrective action.

Recommendation: With the addition of "after-market" splitters, boosters, and other cable enhancing devices, the system may not perform as originally intended. The Builder should not be responsible for any conditions created by "after-market" changes.

<u>GROUNDS</u>

DRAINAGE

WATER DOES NOT DRAIN AWAY FROM FOUNDATION

All soils that surround the foundation of a building should slope a minimum of 1/4-inch fall per every foot of horizontal distance. This required slope must be maintained for a minimum of 5 feet away from the foundation, unless water is diverted from the foundation into an approved structure (such as concrete drainage ditch or graded wale). It is advisable to check slope requirements with the local building department, since several cities, counties, and States require slopes to be more than 2%.

Resolution: At the time of delivery, the Builder must meet the above Requirement.

Recommendation: The Homeowner has a responsibility to always maintain the finish grade and drainage of the property. Homeowners may violate this Guideline in one of two ways: (1) during the installation of landscape materials, they modify the existing grade by leveling it out, causing either a negative slope or a flat slope, or (2) they hire a landscape company that modifies the grade during soils preparation and planting, causing either flat or negative slope. It should also be noted that if gutters and downspouts are not installed, the Homeowner should take it upon themselves to either install them or have them installed. If downspouts are installed, the water should discharge on to approved splash blocks or into a collector system.

IMPROPER SITE DRAINAGE (AREAS BEYOND 5 FEET OF THE PERIMETER OF THE FOUNDATION)

Existing grades and swales are not allowed to drain onto adjoining properties. Water that is transferred via yard drains, swales, or sump pumps may require 48 hours to drain.

Resolution: Builder is responsible for establishing the proper grades prior to the Walkthrough.

Recommendation: The Homeowner is responsible for keeping swales and drains free of slit and other debris.

SETTLING OF SOILS AROUND THE FOUNDATION

Soils that settles and cause water to stand or pond within 5 feet of the foundation perimeter and which does not dissipate within 24 hours after a rain, is considered unacceptable.

Resolution: Soils that surround the foundation should be reasonably compacted in order to meet the above standard.

Recommendation: Any soils that are within the standard should be considered a maintenance issue and corrected by the Homeowner. Erosion occurring during a rainstorm is the responsibility of the Homeowner to repair. NOTE: if the Homeowner modifies the existing grades that surround the foundation which cause the soils to subside in any manner, the Builder should not be held responsible.

SETTLING OF SOILS AT UTILITY TRENCHES

Trenches in landscaped areas should not settle more than 6 inches or cause water to pond within 5 feet of the foundation perimeter. Water that does not dissipate within 24 hours after a rain is considered an unacceptable condition. Trenches that are overlaid with concrete or asphalt are considered unacceptable if water ponds for more than 48 hours after a rain. If a paved over trench subsides more than one inch from the surrounding pavement, it is unacceptable, whether it drains or not.

Resolution: Builder should repair any utility trench condition that does not meet the guideline set forth above.

Recommendation: None.

LANDSCAPING

IMPROPER SOILS PREPARATION

Soils should be prepared according to generally accepted local conditions, as specified by a landscape architect or as recommended by a soils test report.

Resolution: Builder is responsible for reasonable and proper soil preparation in accordance with generally accepted local conditions prior to the planting of materials. This includes placing amendments into high clay soils, etc.

Recommendation: Homeowner should maintain the soils by periodically adding the proper amount of nutrients, i.e. fertilizer, mulch, humus, and minerals required for the particular type of planting.

PLANTS DIE WITHIN THE WARRANTY PERIOD

Any plants that die within the warranty period must be replaced, provided that replacement is not due to improper maintenance or irrigation by the Homeowner.

Resolution: If the Builder furnishes and installs plants, shrubs, trees and/or sod, the Builder should then issue a warranty and maintenance schedule (usually provided by the actual landscape installer) regarding such planted vegetation. This should include the length of warranty and any inclusions and exclusions to said warranty. If any plants die within the warranty period, and is not a result of improper care and/or maintenance by the Homeowner and/or the Homeowners Association, then the Builder should replace any plants that die or appear unhealthy.

Recommendation: The Homeowner or Homeowners Association should supply the required maintenance to ensure that the plants stay healthy. Do not overwater the plants. Any water that is standing (ponding) 30 minutes after watering is a sure sign of overwatering. If there are no specific instructions as to the proper maintenance of the subject plants, then the Homeowner should consult an expert, i.e. nursery, the Builder, or a licensed landscape maintenance contractor. All plants, shrubs, sod and trees should be maintained properly to ensure the healthy growth of the plants.

WEED GROWTH IN LANDSCAPED AREAS

Minimal weed growth is to be expected; "minimal" defined as less than 25% of the planted area.

Resolution: Builder has the responsibility to ensure that proper weed control has been provided prior to planting and immediately after planting.

Recommendation: Homeowners and Homeowners Associations should provide proper maintenance regarding weed control. This may include application of pre-emergent herbicides, spot spraying of contact weed killers and hand weeding.

IRRIGATION

IMPROPER DESIGN AND/OR INSTALLATION OF IRRIGATION SYSTEM

Water should not spray directly onto the building. Minor overspray and wind driven overspray is acceptable. Excessive watering that causes ponding or standing water for more than 24 hours is unacceptable.

Resolution: The irrigation system should be designed to supply the proper amounts of water needed for all landscape (sod, shrubs, and trees) that was installed by the Builder. All irrigation and planting should be according to generally accepted industry standards and local Building Codes. It should be suitable for the geographic region and microclimate, as well.

Recommendation: Homeowner must pay particular attention not to overwater the landscape. Ponding or standing water that accumulates at and around foundations can cause serious structural damage, insect infestation, and plant root rot. Adjusting the watering times on the irrigation controller to avoid overwatering is an important maintenance item. Homeowners Associations, where landscape maintenance is likely to be done by a professional service, overwatering may be commonplace.

CONTROLLER/CLOCK DOES NOT OPERATE

The landscape irrigation controller/clock should operate as intended by the manufacturer within the warranty period.

Resolution: Builder shall repair or replace the controller/clock if it falls within the warranty period.

Recommendation: Change the backup battery (if the controller has one) once a year.

RETAINING WALLS

WALL LEAKS

Water that leaks or migrates through the wall is unacceptable, except through weep holes that are intentionally designed for that purpose.

Resolution: Builder should make any and all repairs necessary to meet the above guideline.

Recommendation: It is important for the Homeowner to maintain the method for surface water to be diverted away from the wall either through a concrete swale or berm. Homeowner should also try and identify where the trench drain (providing that one has been installed) daylights (daylight refers to the end of the drain pipe that is visible) in order to determine whether or not the drain system is clogged during heavy rains.

CRACKS IN WALLS AND MORTAR JOINTS

Cracks greater than 1/4-inch are considered unacceptable

Resolution: Builder should make the repairs as necessary, provided that the Homeowner has not modified the slope above the retaining wall.

Recommendation: Homeowner has a responsibility to repair any cracks that are within the guideline (anything up to 1/4- inch) in a timely fashion. On long slopes that are relatively steep, surface water should also be diverted away from the top of the wall to prevent conditions that could lead to cracking.

WHITE CHALK-LIKE SUBSTANCE APPEARS ON THE FACE OF THE WALL

This is a normal condition and is considered acceptable.

Resolution: Builder is not responsible for common efflorescence. However, if there is severe efflorescence (where the entire face of the wall has a coating of white powder), this condition should be investigated further. If there is a large recurring area, there is the possibility that the waterproofing membrane has been installed improperly, or is possibly missing. It may also be possible that a sub-drain is failing or missing.

Recommendation: Common efflorescence is easily removed by brushing or by a high pressure water spray.

WALL IS OUT OF PLUMB

Walls should not exceed 3/4-inch out of plumb in a 6-foot vertical direction.

Resolution: Builder should make the necessary repairs to meet the above guideline. Builder should replace all landscape materials damaged in the repair process.

Recommendation: None, providing that the Homeowner has not built something on top of the wall or altered the slope in a way that would compromise the design of the wall.

FENCING

WOOD POSTS, PICKETS OR PANELS ARE ROTTING

Posts should be made of pressure-treated wood, heartwood of cedar, or redwood. Bottom rails and pickets or sideboards should maintain a minimum clearance of 2 inches to finished grade. Posts should be set in concrete above grade so that water does not accumulate against the post.

Resolution: Builder should furnish a completed fence with the appropriate clearance between wood and finished grade. If the fence (railings, pickets or siding) is in contact with the finished grade, Builder should make the repairs necessary.

Recommendation: Homeowner should not change the finished grade in any way that would affect the above guideline. If natural conditions (i.e. rains washed soils down onto the fence) cause the guideline to be compromised, it is the Homeowner's responsibility to make the appropriate corrections. Planting shrubs whose foliage is in constant contact with the fence may also potentially reduce the life of the fence boards.

FENCING IS PREMATURELY WEATHERED OR RUSTED

Wood fences are expected to weather unless they are painted at the time of installation. Thereafter they become a Homeowner maintenance item.

Resolution: Wrought iron or ornamental iron fences should be completely painted upon installation. All weld joints must be painted.

Recommendation: Do not allow irrigation sprinklers to spray directly onto the fence. It is recommended to paint or seal a wood fence every three years. Wrought iron fences should be inspected semi-annually and painted whenever rust is evident.

WARPS, KNOTS AND CRACKS EXIST IN FENCE BOARDS

Fence boards that have loose or dislodged knots covering more than 25% of the width of the board are considered unacceptable. Boards that are split top to bottom and where the split is 3/8-inch wide are considered unacceptable. Boards that warp more than one inch in 6 feet of length are considered unacceptable.

Resolution: Builder should replace boards that do not meet the above criteria.

Recommendation: Homeowner should keep the fence in good repair by periodic re-nailing of loose boards. Painting and sealing wood fences will prolong their useful life.

MISCELLANEOUS

ICE AND SNOW

ROOF SAFE OR FAILS UNDER SNOW LOAD

Roofs should not fail under normal snow loads for the region; roofs may sag or deflect by only the amount permitted under the local Code.

Resolution: Be certain before starting construction that snow load requirements for the local area are met. Builder shall make necessary repairs if the above requirement is not met.

Recommendation: During periods of exceptionally heavy snowfall, it is likely that accumulations of snow will have to be removed from the roof. Except in isolated areas, there are companies that perform this service.

DOORS AND WINDOWS ARE BLOCKED WITH SNOW

This is a Homeowner maintenance issue.

Resolution: Builder has no responsibility.

Recommendation: When garage doors, access doors and windows become blocked, it is up to the Homeowner to take preventative measures to keep repetition of these problems to a minimum. The severity of this condition tends to depend upon local geographic location, House design and orientation to the weather conditions.

ICE DAMS CAUSE EAVES TO LEAK

Ice dams should not cause eaves to leak

Resolution: Construct the House in conformance to the requirements of the Building Code and local Code amendments with respect to ice dam elimination. Make necessary corrections if ice dams persist under normal weather conditions. If a structural or other type of failure occurs because of extreme weather conditions, the Builder is not responsible.

Recommendation: Become aware of the causes of ice dams and the preventative steps that can be taken. Keep gutters, drains, deck openings and major catch basins free of debris and other obstructions. If there are publicly owned drainage facilities nearby that are subject to blockage, do not hesitate to contact authorities to request maintenance. Failure to do this could result in localized flooding during periods of rapid snowmelt, with consequent property damage.

NOISE TRANSMISSION

SOUNDS CAN BE HEARD THROUGH WALLS AND FLOORS

1. Party walls (also referred to as common walls) and floors between units: Sound transmission must be limited by Code to meet a Sound Transmission Coefficient (STC) Standard of 50. Measurement of sound transmission can only be made using specialized equipment. The STC Standard of 50 is a laboratory test standard. When approved wall or floor assembly is tested in the field, an STC rating of 45 is considered acceptable.
2. Devices (fans, etc.) should be of the quiet operating type; water and plumping waste lines should be installed in a manner that minimizes transmission of noise directly from pipes to the structure of the building.
3. At interior walls and ceilings: insulate vertical waste lines; use sound absorbing underlayment at floors (particularly hard surfaces such as tile and uncovered hardwood floors) when units on different floors are not under control of the same owner.

4. The Performance Guideline regarding noise transmission between walls and floors of detached single-family homes is that the occupants of detached houses can control their own noise level.

Resolution: Builder should correct any deviations from STC standards where identified. Inform the Homeowner that it is impossible to totally eliminate noise transmission in party walls and common floor housing.

Recommendation: Avoid any changes that affect the assembly of sound-insulating party walls or ceilings; avoid making new openings in walls and floors. A common Homeowner error is to install a stereophonic speaker system in the party walls of a townhouse or condominium.

MOLD AND MILDEW

MOLD AND MILDEW GROWTH WHERE LEAKS OCCUR

No condition should be permitted to exist, such as a rainwater leak, plumbing leak, or use of excessively wet framing lumber, which fosters the growth of mold and mildew.

Resolution: Builder shall perform repairs of leaks caused by Builder as necessary to eliminate sources of water intrusion. Remove and arrest the growth of mold and mildew.

Recommendation: Homeowner is responsible for promptly addressing any instances of leakage, and if Builder caused, reporting to the Builder any instances of leakage, so that preventative repairs can be accomplished before significant damage occurs. If leaks are corrected quickly, mold and mildew may not flourish, and repairs and clean-ups are much easier to accomplish.

MOLD AND MILDEW GROWTH AROUND WINDOWS, DOORS, BASEBOARDS, BATHROOM SURFACES, ABSENT OF OBVIOUS LEAKS

No condition should be created, as a result of construction practices, so as to foster the growth of molds or mildews. Absent of leaks, this is a Homeowner maintenance item.

Resolution: Repair any conditions that may result from improper construction that cause mold and mildew growth.

Recommendation: Showers and tubs should be routinely cleaned and dried after each use and window frames and joints should be periodically cleaned in order to prevent mold and mildew growth. If mildew or mold is observed, use of mildewcide (available at any cleaning supply or hardware store) to prevent and retard any regrowth. In addition, it is helpful to air out rooms on a frequent basis. Ensure that all exhaust fans and other air circulation devices are functioning properly and used routinely. Do not install air deflectors over heat supply grills. Open draperies often during rainy periods to allow air to circulate around windows. Limit the use of atomizers or humidifiers. Windows should be open or vent fans should be operating at all times while showering or bathing. Window tracks and weep holes should be cleaned at least twice yearly to prevent mold and mildew.

MILDEW GROWTH ON SIDING, STUCCO AND OTHER EXTERIOR SURFACES

1) The installation of siding should be made so that it prevents water from entering behind siding
2) The design and location of buildings on the site that are clad in hardboard of OSB siding should provide for adequate exposure to sunlight and ventilation, and should avoid unusually damp surroundings
3) Interior spaces should be adequately ventilated and protected by vapor barriers to avoid excessive condensation build-up that may result in the growth of mildew, mold and fungi.

Resolution: Once the Builder has met the above guideline, there is little the Builder can do to prevent mold and mildew from occurring on outside walls. Variations in orientation, weather and the spore count in the air can all have an effect on the growth of mold and mildew on exterior walls.

Recommendation: Keep siding sealed and painted. Avoid spraying siding and stucco with landscape sprinklers. If mold and mildew grows on outside walls, take prompt action. Use of mildew-killing sprays and brushing with water and soap can arrest or reverse mildew conditions. The Homeowner should also avoid panting shrubbery that will block sunlight and ventilation from siding. Do not allow ivy or other vine plants to grow on siding and keep existing shrubbery pruned back from siding.

MILDEW OR MOLD GROWTH IN HEATING AND VENTILATION DUCT WORK

The design and installation of heating and ventilating ductwork should be accomplished in a manner that does not encourage the growth of organisms within the enclosed system.

Resolution: Builder is responsible for installing a properly assembled and insulated heating and ventilating system and repairing conditions resulting from improper installation.

Recommendation: Notify the Builder promptly of any suspected problem of this nature

MOLD OR MILDEW GROWTH NEAR ENCLOSED PLUMPING PIPES

Cold water pipes in wall cavities and other interior spaces subject to moist, warm air should be insulated.

Resolution: Builder should install pipe insulation on cold water pipes where there is a likelihood of condensation and mold growth.

Recommendation: None.

SEPTIC TANKS

SEWER SYSTEM / DRAINS NOT OPERATING PROPERLY

All septic or waste systems should be capable of operating as designed, under normal use without any stoppage or back up.

Resolution: At time of delivery of the House, the Builder should demonstrate that the septic system is operating as designed. If a clogged sewer line/drain is the result of improper installation by the Builder, then the Builder should repair the non-performing condition. The Builder will not be held accountable for sewers and drains that are clogged because of Homeowner negligence or misuse.

Recommendation: The tank should be pumped out every 2-3 years, depending on the size of the system and the number of people that live in the household. The local health department may require more frequent pumping. The following items are examples of Homeowner negligence regarding septic tanks:

- Pouring paint thinners, pesticides, motor oils, or chemicals down drains or in toilets.
- Disposing of grease, fat, paper towels, or feminine sanitary products in toilets.
- Drain cleaners should be used with caution and sparingly (drain cleaners kill bacteria that break down sewage).
- Use of dyed toilet tissue (dyes are harmful to the bacteria in the tank).

SEPTIC TANK EMITS FOUL ODOR

Septic tanks should not emit unreasonably foul odors, given proper Homeowner use and maintenance.

Resolution: Builder has no responsibility.

Recommendation: Keep the tank pumped out on a regular basis. Periodically adds a bacteria-enhancing agent (sold at any hardware store). If the number of persons using the system increases, consider expanding the system.

SMOKE DETECTORS

DIRECTORS SOUND DURING USE OF FIREPLACE / KITCHEN

Smoke detectors are designed to be smoke sensitive; this is for the protection of the occupants. In all likelihood when smoke detectors sound at the time of cooking, the room has been overloaded with cooking vapors. If the detector sounds each time a fire is built in the fireplace, there may be ventilation problem.

Resolution: The Builder is responsible for installing a Code-complaint detector system. If the detectors sound at inappropriate times, and the fault lies with poorly constructed ventilation systems, the Builder should correct the non-performing condition.

Recommendation: The Homeowner should operate fireplaces and cook in a manner that does not cause undue quantities of smoke to be generated within the House.

DETECTORS DO NOT OPERATE WHEN TESTED

All smoke detector should operate as intended by Code, and in compliance with manufacturer's specifications. Smoke detectors that do not operate because the battery is dead are considered a Homeowner maintenance item.

Resolution: In the event of a malfunctioning detector, the Builder should conduct an investigation to determine the cause, and should take corrective action as appropriate to restore function.

Recommendation: Homeowners should test detectors once a month using the test button on the detector. All newly installed detector systems operate from the house electrical, as well as a battery back-up. The Homeowner must make sure the batteries are changed on a regular basis so the back-up system will function in the event of a power failure. It is a good idea to change all of the batteries at the same time, even though just one detector is signaling a low battery beep. Another good idea is to write the date of the change of the batteries on a piece of tape on each battery. If one detector consistently uses more battery power than others, then it may be defective. If that is the case, it is important that the defective detector be replaced.

BIBLIOGRAPHY AND REFERENCES

American Concrete Institute. (2011). *ACI 318-Building Code Requirements for Structural Concrete*. Farmington Hills, MI.

American Concrete Institute. (2011). *ACI 530- Building Code Requirements for Masonry Structures*. Farmington Hills, MI.

American Forest and Paper Association. (2011) *Wood Frame Construction Manual for One- and Two-Family Dwellings (WFCM)*. Leesburg, VA.

American Iron and Steel Institute. (2007). *Standard for Cold-Formed Steel Framing—Prescriptive Method for One - and Two-Family Dwellings (AISI S230)*. Washington D.C.

American Society of Heating, Refrigerating and Air-Conditioning Engineers. (2006-2009). *ASHRAE Handbook: Fundamentals*. Atlanta, GA.

Ballast, D. (1994). *Handbook of Construction Tolerances*. McGraw Hill.

Building Industry Association of San Diego County. (1993). *Top 25 Construction Problems and Their Resolution*. Construction Quality Task Force.

California Building Industry Association. (2005). *SB 800, The Homebuilder "FIX IT" Construction Dispute Resolution Law*. Sacramento, CA.

California, State of, Department of Real Estate. (1996). *Operating Cost Manual for Homeowner Association*. Sacramento, CA.

California, State of, Contractor's State License Board. (1982). *Workmanship Guidelines*. Sacramento, CA.

Concrete Committee of San Diego County. (2001). *Concrete Performance Standards and Maintenance guidelines*. San Diego, CA.

Gypsum Association. (2012). *Fire Resistance Design Manual*. Hyattsville, MD.

Hansen, D. & Kardon, R. (2011). *Code Check – Building*. Taunton Press. Newtown, CT.

Hansen, D. & Kardon, R. (2010). *Code Check – Electrical*. Taunton Press. Newtown, CT.

Hansen, D. & Kardon, R. (2011). *Code Check – Plumbing & Mechanical.* Taunton Press. Newtown, CT.

International Code Council. (2007). *California Building Code.* Whittier, CA.

International Code Council. (2007). *California Electrical Code.* Whittier, CA.

International Code Council. (2007). *California Mechanical Code.* Whittier, CA.

International Code Council. (2007). *California Plumbing Code.* Whittier, CA.

International Code Council. (2006-2009). *International Residential Code for One and Two Family Dwellings.* Washington D.C.

International Association of Plumbing & Mechanical Officials. (2009). *Uniform Mechanical Code.* Ontario, CA.

International Association of Plumbing & Mechanical Officials. (2009). *Uniform Plumbing Code.* Ontario, CA.

Journal of Light Construction. (1997). *Troubleshooting Guide to Residential Construction*, Builderburg Group.

NAHM Research Center, Inc. (2001). *Mold in Residential Buildings.* Washington D.C.

National Association of State Contracting Licensing Agencies. (2009). *NASCLA Residential Construction Standards.* Phoenix, AZ.

National Fire Protection Association. (2011). *National Electrical Code.*

National Roofing Contractor's Association. (2007-1009). *NCRA Roofing and Waterproofing Manual.* Vols 1, 2, & 3. Rosemont, IL.

National Wood Flooring Association. (2000). *Problems, Causes and Cures.* Ellisville, MO.

NAHB Home Builder Press. (2005). *Residential Construction Performance Guidelines.* Washington D.C.

New Jersey, State of, Division of Codes and Standards. (2005). *Homeowners booklet*, New Home Warranty Program. NJ.

Reynolds, D. (1998). *Residential & Light Commercial Construction Standards*. R.S. Means, Inc. Kingston, MA.

Sacks, A. (1994). *Residential Water Problems*. NAHM Home Builder Press. Washington, DC.

Structural Building Component Association & Truss Plate Institute. (2006-2013). *Guide to Good Practice for Handling, Installing, Restraining & Bracing of Metal Plate Connected Wood Trusses*.

Tenebaum, D. (1996). *The Complete Idiot's Guide to Trouble Free Home Repair*. Alpha Books. NY.

Truss Plate Institute. (2008). *National Design Standard for Metal Plate Connected Wood Truss Construction*. Alexandria, VA.

ABOUT THE AUTHOR

Ryan Brautovich is an Army veteran with more than 20 years of home construction, home remodeling and building experience who has consulted for Fortune 500 home builders as well as the Top 100 privately held home building companies. He is a custom home builder in California and a California licensed general contractor. Ryan is International Code Council Certified, an International and California Building Inspector as well as an International and California Plumbing Inspector. He is a graduate of Auburn University with degrees in both Accounting and Business Management. He has consulted for the City of Lancaster (CA) Building & Safety Department, K. Hovnanian Homes, Beezer Homes, Pardee Homes, KB Homes, Standard Pacific Homes, American Premiere Homes, Richmond American Homes, DR Horton, and Frontier Homes – just to name a few.

Ryan founded the Construction H.E.L.P. Foundation, a national nonprofit organization, dedicated to advocating for and meeting the needs of individuals who have suffered at the hands of unscrupulous contractors and sub-contractors who simply took advantage of the helpless homeowner in order to make a quick buck – and either didn't finish the project, overcharged or simply took money and didn't perform the work as promised. Over the years, the number of phone calls Ryan received increased dramatically from frustrated and angry homeowners who were desperately seeking help after being ripped off by other contractors. As a result, he founded the Construction H.E.L.P. Foundation, and it's educational assistance program – Home Construction Audit – to provide assistance and education to homeowners. As the founder of the Construction H.E.L.P. Foundation, Ryan has made it the organization's daily mission to return ethics to the home building and home remodeling profession and provide homeowners with the expert help and crucial knowledge they need so that they will never be taken advantage of again.

www.ingramcontent.com/pod-product-compliance
Lightning Source LLC
Chambersburg PA
CBHW021129300426
44113CB00006B/354